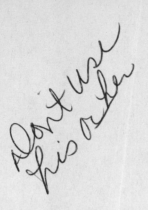

Action-Grammar

Fast, No-Hassle Answers on Everyday Usage and Punctuation

Joanne Feierman

A FIRESIDE BOOK
Published by Simon & Schuster
New York   London   Toronto   Sydney   Tokyo   Singapore

F

FIRESIDE
Rockefeller Center
1230 Avenue of the Americas
New York, NY 10020

FIRESIDE and colophon are registered trademarks of Simon & Schuster Inc.

Designed by Irving Perkins Associates

Manufactured in the United States of America

10   9   8   7   6   5

Library of Congress Cataloging-in-Publication Data

Feierman, Joanne.
    ActionGrammar : fast, no-hassle answers on everyday usage and
punctuation / Joanne Feierman.
        p.   cm.
    Includes bibliographical references and index.
    (alk. paper)
    1. English language—Grammar—Handbooks, manuals, etc. 2. English
language—Punctuation—Handbooks, manuals, etc. 3. English
language—Usage—Handbooks, manuals, etc. I. Title.
PE1112.F395   1995
808'.042'076—dc20   95-22955
                                                                          CIP

ISBN 0–684–80780–7

For Martin—who lights up my life.

Acknowledgments

Many thanks to Barbara and Michael Stedman and to Dick and Faith Evans, whose help and love have enriched this book and my life. I am also indebted to my children, Alex and Rachel, for their advice on this manuscript and their ability to live with a grammar grump for long stretches of time; to my father, Nathan Kollin, for his suggestions; and to Jessica Feierman, Mariah Motley, David Shields, Erica Kaplan, Eric Johnson, Joel Kollin, Jeanette Sheinman, Steven Feierman, Sandy Barnes, and Bonnie GraBois for their help and support. Special thanks to my editor, Becky Cabaza, for her wise guidance.

Contents

Introduction

> A generation ago I knew the rules—knew them by heart, word for word, though not their meanings—and I still know them: the one which says—which says—but never mind, it will come back to me presently.
>
> —MARK TWAIN ON GRAMMAR

If you're like most people I've met in my business writing courses, you want your writing to look and sound right. You want to use the right words and feel confident you've got the commas in the right places. But like Mark Twain, you seem to have forgotten, or never learned, those grammar rules. So when you're stumped by a grammar issue, you pull down that big dictionary or grammar book from the shelf and start searching. Usually the search ends with your feeling more confused than enlightened, lost in a spin of grammar terms that only an English teacher could love.

If this sounds familiar, *ActionGrammar* is for you.

This book is designed to help you even if you can't remember transitive verbs and couldn't pick out a preposition in a police lineup. It speaks plain English.* It doesn't talk in English-

---

*Actually we do use a few grammatical terms, but we define these in plain English in the Glossary on pages 239–42.

teacher jargon or spend time on esoteric grammar issues that you need to know once every ten years. It covers only the business and everyday writing issues that most of us need to know to get our ideas on paper (or out of our mouths) clearly and correctly.

If you doubt that a book this small could contain everything you need to know to write correctly, consider the dictionary. My *Random House Unabridged Dictionary* has 2,477 pages of very small print and weighs nine pounds. But a dictionary in the same small print containing the words regularly used by a college graduate would come to only a hundred pages and weigh less than a pound.

Just as you don't need to know every word in an unabridged dictionary to speak well, you don't need to learn every rule in a freshman college grammar book to write well. But you do need to know the basics: the issues that come up every day. And that's just what you'll find in this little book.

So master the information in it and get rid of the grammar ghost that looks over your shoulder as you write and keeps you from being the best writer you can be.

How to Use This Book

To get the most from this book, begin by taking the Language Challenge (*challenge* is a nicer word than *quiz*) on page 20 of Chapter 2, "Mistakes Your Boss Minds the Most." The challenge will let you know whether you are making mistakes in speaking or writing that managers and executives find disturbing. Remember, poor grammar is like dandruff: Everyone wants to tell you you've got it, everyone intends to tell you you've got it, but no one will. The Language Challenge is your chance to find out. (The challenge is followed by an answer key that gives the correct answer and tells you where in the book you can find more information about that grammar, punctuation, or usage issue.)

If you passed the Language Challenge with flying colors, turn to Part Five, "Mastering Business Writing," for suggestions on how to write clear, concise letters, memos, and E-mail. Putting the guidelines to work will enable you to produce business writing that not only communicates a message but communicates the right message about you.

Then put this book in a handy spot so you can use it whenever you're not sure where a comma goes, whether a sentence that ends in *a.m.* requires an additional period, or whether the correct word is *assure, ensure,* or *insure.*

If you did not do well on the Language Challenge, you should focus on Part Two, which tells you how to put punctuation marks in their correct places, and Part Three, which deals with what grammarians call the mechanics—how to write numbers, spell, capitalize, and abbreviate correctly, and how to hyphenate words that come at the end of a line of writing. Part Four is the heavy-duty section on grammar; it tackles the difficult issues. Part Five offers up some everyday advice on mastering business writing.

Each chapter begins with a challenge that allows you to pinpoint the information you need to study in that chapter. Once you see which items you've missed, you can go directly to the pages indicated, bypassing the material you already have under control.

Don't forget the Appendix. It contains a list of frequently misspelled words, sixty-four simple business verbs that you will find very useful, layouts for letters and memos, and dozens of words that are often confused and abused, like *affect* and *effect, already* and *all ready, disinterested* and *uninterested.* This book is designed to tell you what you need to know and to provide some smiles along the way. Enjoy!

Who Makes Up the Rules?

As you thumb through this book, you'll see that each rule is followed by examples labeled *correct* or *incorrect, preferred* or *acceptable.* Like most people, you've probably wondered who makes up these rules. Who decides what's correct and what's incorrect? Who has decided that *irregardless* is always wrong and that *between you and I* is unacceptable? After all, we hear these expressions frequently.

If this were a book on French grammar, I'd have no trouble telling you who makes up the rules. The French have an official body called the French Academy that decides what is acceptable and what is not. They rule on matters of grammar, punctuation, usage, and even spelling, and all government publications and schools must follow their decrees. (One of the things that really annoy the academy is the number of English words that have crept into everyday French. Therefore, they've banned the use of words like *le software* and *le weekend* from all official publications.)

But in the United States, things are much more complicated. We have no such body and we never will; we're much too democratic for that. We have many authorities on grammar—professors and teachers of English, writers, and linguists—who write dictionaries and grammar textbooks. The problem is that these authorities don't always agree with one another. To make matters worse, they change their mind. In high school I was taught that you could never, ever begin a sentence with the word *and* or *but*. Now *Harbrace College Handbook,* one of the best-selling college grammar texts, *suggests* that we begin sentences with *and* or *but* to make our sentences more interesting. And, in fact, writers of the country's finest newspapers and magazines often begin sentences with *and* and *but*. (If you'd like to know more about rules of yesterday that are no more, you'll enjoy reading Chapter 1, "Five Lies Your English Teacher Told You.")

ActionGrammar brings you up to date on all the important issues, pointing out the hard-and-fast rules and those on which the authorities don't agree. When there are several acceptable ways to handle a grammar, punctuation, or usage issue, we explain the options so you can make an educated choice.

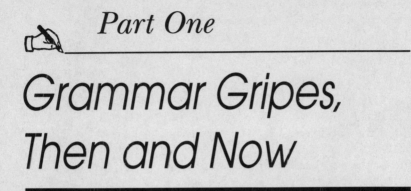

Part One

Grammar Gripes, Then and Now

1 *Five Lies Your English Teacher Told You*

That sure is a great school. It's practical.
They don't teach no goddamn grammar
there.

—A KANSAS FARMER, QUOTED BY

NELSON ANTRIM CRAWFORD, C. 1914

Well, I'm exaggerating. Your English teacher didn't tell you lies. But she or he probably taught you rules of English that are no more.

Were you taught any of the "rules" below? If you were, read this chapter.

1. You may not start a sentence with *because.*
2. You may not start a sentence with *and* or *but.*
3. Sometimes periods and commas go inside the quotation marks and sometimes they go outside; it depends on the sentence.
4. You may not end a sentence with a preposition.
5. You may not split an infinitive.

Here is the most up-to-date information on these issues.

1. You may not start a sentence with *because*.

You certainly may. This much-believed "rule" has never been found in any book of grammar!

Let's examine:

> I made $100,000 on a stock because I got a great tip.

> Because I got a great tip, I made $100,000 on a stock.

Both of these sentences are absolutely, positively correct.

If this is true, why do you and I remember being told, in no uncertain terms, that you can't start a sentence with *because*? The answer is this: Teachers in primary grades wanted to instill in their students the habit of writing and speaking in *full* sentences, not sentence fragments.

If your teacher asked, "Why did you make $100,000 on a stock?" and you answered, "Because I got a great tip," she would most likely say, "You can't start a sentence with *because*." What she should have said was, "Please make that a complete sentence." *Because I got a great tip* is a cliff-hanger; it's a sentence fragment and needs to be finished. But instead, she just said, "You can't start a sentence with *because*."

Indeed, the teacher told you a white lie. As a result, people write wordy, awkward sentences like this:

> Due to the fact that I got a great tip, I made $100,000 on a stock.

[You'll find more about *due to* and *because* on page 199.]

2. You may not start a sentence with *and* or *but*.

False. Good writers do it all the time. Take a look at *The New York Times, The Wall Street Journal,* or any other major publication; you'll see many sentences that start with *and, but,* and even *so*!

The same thing that happened to *because* happened to *and, but,* and *so.* Your teachers were afraid you would write sentences like these:

> I look forward to seeing you next week. And completing the contract by the first of July.

And completing the contract by the first of July is not a sentence and can't stand alone.

However, to write *And I hope we can complete the contract by the first of July* would be perfectly fine. This starts with *and,* yet it contains a complete sentence: *I hope we can complete the contract by the first of July.*

Of course, many other correct sentences could have been written to communicate the same thought. Here are some:

1. I look forward to seeing you next week and completing the contract by the first of July.

2. I look forward to seeing you next week; I hope we can complete the contract by the first of July.

3. I look forward to seeing you next week, and I hope we can complete the contract by the first of July.

4. I look forward to seeing you next week. I hope we can complete the contract by the first of July.

3. Sometimes periods and commas go inside the quotation marks and sometimes they go outside; it depends on the sentence.

No—well, at least not in America. In the United States, periods and commas always go inside quotation marks. That's our rule, and it is followed scrupulously by all professional writers.

Therefore, all of the following are correct:

1. The vice president said, "We will have to review our objectives for the project." (Here the quoted material is a complete sentence.)

2. Although the letter addressed to my supervisor was stamped "Personal and Confidential," I took it to my office and read it. (Here the quoted material is just three words. The comma is required to indicate a pause.)

3. My manager described his assistant's behavior as "inappropriate." (The quoted material is just one word.)

Do I hear an objection? Did you say our rule makes no sense? After all, in example two the letter was stamped "Personal and Confidential" and not "Personal and Confidential,"—and therefore, you ask, shouldn't the comma come *after* the quotation marks? Well, I agree with you, but that is not the rule.

And what about the third example? Only one word is quoted. Does the period still go inside? The answer is yes. This is the American system. The rest of the English-speaking world uses the more logical system, as do publications of international bodies such as the United Nations. The only Americans who do not follow the American style in this matter are lawyers.

For more information on this issue, see Rule 10, page 72.

4. You may not end a sentence with a preposition.

Much has been written on this topic—in fact, too much has been written about it. The story is told that Winston Churchill was once criticized for using a sentence that ended with a preposition. He was angry; he responded: "That is the kind of English up with which I will not put." His meaning is clear: Don't rework a sentence into a totally awkward one to avoid ending a sentence with a preposition. Not ending a sentence with a preposition is a guideline, not a rule.

Yes, generally speaking, you should not end sentences with prepositions because they are dull, weak words (words like *of, with, to, at, in*). You should end sentences with powerful words. Notice the difference:

> This is the report I want to talk with you about.

> I want to talk with you about this report.

The second sentence is clearer and more forceful.

However, don't follow this rule slavishly or you may end up, as the prime minister pointed out, with a sentence that's awkward and confusing:

> This is the report about which I want to talk with you.

5. You may not split an infinitive.

An infinitive is the word *to* plus a verb, for example, *to review, to explain, to understand*. In the following sentence, the infinitive, *to review*, is split by the word *carefully*.

Frowned upon:
> Her responsibility was to carefully review the data.

Favored:
> Her responsibility was to review the data carefully.

Do not split an infinitive unless *not* doing so leads to a confusing or awkward sentence. In the following examples, the sentence with the split infinitive is preferable to the unsplit ones because it's the clearest; it puts the emphasis in the right spot.

Clearest and best:
> I would like you to personally supervise the clerk.

Awkward:
> I would like you personally to supervise the clerk.

Okay:
> I would like you to supervise the clerk personally.

2 Mistakes Your Boss Minds the Most

> No passion in the world is equal to the passion to alter someone else's draft.
>
> —H. G. WELLS

Over the past fifteen years I've interviewed executives and asked them to list their top ten pet language peeves. I've learned two things in the process: First, people care about language use. The people I spoke with needed only a moment to think of errors in writing and speaking that really bothered them. And they were quite passionate about the whole issue. "Please be sure to put that in your book," they said. No one, in response to my question, said "Oh, nothing I can think of."

Second, the same mistakes were mentioned over and over again. That's good news, because by mastering the items in this chapter, you will at least have conquered the major issues.

Language Challenge: Top Ten Errors in Speaking and Writing

Here are the top ten errors. The first five are frequently heard in conversation, and the next five are frequently seen in writing. I've also included one special mention. See if you can identify the errors and the corrections. The answers follow.

1. I'm going to speak with him irregardless of what you say.
2. Let's keep this information just between you and I.
3. The software runs good on this computer.
4. Just leave the problem to Frank and myself.
5. Me and him are working on that now.
6. In the quarterly report, Ms. Conway said that sales of the new product were "disappointing".
7. The new legislation will effect our taxes.
8. The meeting was attended by Carol, Barbara, and myself.
9. According to my secretary, its too late to make changes.
10. We had wanted to wait until September to make a decision, however, we decided to act now.

Special Mention Award

Well, basically, I think we've sort of got the problem, you know, under control.

Answers to Language Challenge

1. I'm going to speak with him irregardless of what you say.

Correction:
There is no such word as *irregardless.* Use *regardless* instead.

Reason: Regardless means *without regard.* If you add an *ir* to a word, you change the word to its opposite. *Irregular* is the opposite of *regular, irresponsible* is the opposite of *responsible,* so *irregardless* would mean the opposite of *without regard,* which would be *with regard,* which you don't mean. Oh well, take my word for it: *Irregardless* is not a word.

2. Let's keep this information just between you and I.

Correction:

Never use this expression. It is always *between you and me.*

Reason: The rules of grammar dictate that the word *between* must always be followed by *me*, never *I.*

Therefore, say—

Come sit between Susan and me.

I want you to keep this information between you and me.

Between you and me, I got a great new job!

If you want to know more about *me* and *I*, see Chapter 11, "Pronoun Problems," page 125.

3. The software runs good on this computer.

Correction:

The correct word is *well.*

Reason: Well, not *good,* describes how things work. Whenever you want to explain how things operate, how they do something, how an action is done, use *well.*

Remember, *well* answers questions that start with *how*—

My brother speaks *well.* (How does he *speak?* Well.)

We did *well* on our first group presentation. (How did we *do?* Well.)

I will do *well* on the test. (How will I *do?* Well.)

I thought the project went *well.* (How did I think the project *went?* Well.)

You'll find out more about *well* and *good* on page 212.

4. Just leave the problem to Frank and myself.

Correction:
Replace *myself* with *me.*

Reason: To determine the correct word, say the sentence without the words *Frank and.* You will then automatically supply the correct word. (Just leave the problem to *me.*)

For more about when to use *me, myself,* and *I,* see Chapter 11, "Pronoun Problems," page 125.

5. Me and him are working on that now.

Correction:
Replace *me* with *I,* and *him* with *he.* Switch the order: *He and I are working on that now.*

Reason: To determine the correct word, create two sentences: *I am working on that now. He is working on that now.* Then combine the sentences, but put yourself last. (It's not polite to mention yourself first.) *He and I are working on that now.*

For more information about *me, myself,* and *I,* see Chapter 11, "Pronoun Problems," page 125.

6. In the quarterly report, Ms. Conway said that sales of the new product were "disappointing".

Correction:
In the quarterly report, Ms. Conway said that sales of the new product were *"disappointing."*

Reason: Periods always belong inside the quotation marks in the United States.

To learn more about how to handle quotation marks when they occur with commas, semicolons, colons, question marks, and exclamation marks, see Rules 10–13, pages 72, 73.

7. The new legislation will effect our taxes.

Correction:
Change *effect* to *affect*.

Reason: To *affect* means to *do something to*. An *effect* is a *result*. Substitute each meaning in the sentence and select the one that makes sense.
Which makes sense?

The new legislation will *result* our taxes.

The new legislation will *do something to* our taxes.

The second is better; therefore, the correct choice is *affect*. For a more in-depth explanation of *affect* and *effect*, see page 192.

8. The meeting was attended by Carol, Barbara, and myself.

Correction:
Change *myself* to *me*.

Reason: To determine the correct word, say the sentence without the words *Carol, Barbara, and*. You will then automatically supply the correct word. (The meeting was attended by *me*.)
Carol, Barbara, and I attended the meeting is also correct.
For more about *myself* and *me*, see Chapter 11, "Pronoun Problems," page 125.

9. According to my secretary, its too late to make changes.

Correction:
Change *its* to *it's*.

Reason: *It's* means *it is*. *Its* means *belonging to it*. (Example: *Put the file in its proper folder.*)
For more help in understanding apostrophes, see page 74.

10. We had wanted to wait until September to make a decision, however, we decided to act now.

Correction:

Replace the comma before *however* with a semicolon.

Reason: When *however* is used to glue two sentences together—as it is here—a semicolon must be used before *however* and a comma after it.

The sentence could also be written this way: *We wanted to wait until September to make a decision. However, we decided to act now.*

To learn more about the different ways in which *however* is punctuated, see page 46.

Special Mention Award: overuse of the words basically, like, you know, sort of, *and* kind of

> Well, basically, I think we've sort of got the problem, you know, under control.

Technically, this sentence is not wrong, but it is dreadfully boring. It's full of dead words—*well, basically, I think, you know*—and the waffle words *sort of*. These expressions suck the power out of your speech and thus make you sound unsure of yourself. Compare the above sentence with *I've got the problem under control.* (Of course, if you're *not* sure, just say, *I think I've got the problem under control.*)

What should you say in place of *basically,* and so forth? *Nothing.* Absolutely nothing. When someone asks you a question, collect your thoughts: Don't say *basically* or *well*—think! Then speak. A pause—even in midsentence—is more powerful than any filler word.

Unfortunately, you won't know if you use these verbal fillers, since those who use them don't hear themselves saying them. The only way to check is to tape yourself in conversation and listen to see if you sprinkle your speech with verbal fillers.

Twenty More Language Pet Peeves— and the Answers

Here are twenty more usage and grammar errors plus twenty words that are frequently mispronounced. The answers follow.

1. Please give Bob and I an opportunity to bid on the project. (Pages 126, 127, 128, 129.)
2. I felt badly for him. (Pages 198, 199.)
3. Where's he at? (Page 197.)
4. The reason is because we were late. (Page 223.)
5. Being as I am new here, I don't know the answer. (Page 200.)
6. As per our conversation, the credit has not yet been issued. (Page 196.)
7. Our objectives are to: purchase the new system by January 1, install it by March 1, and begin training the staff on March 15. (Rule 6, Danger, page 68.)
8. There's many reasons why the strategy won't work. (Rule 14, pages 141, 142.)
9. We must discuss this farther when we meet next week. (Pages 210, 211.)
10. He's real well informed on that topic. (Page 223.)
11. I spoke with Cindy in regards to the contract. (Page 215.)
12. We've got less phone lines than we used to have. (Page 211.)
13. I informed him as to the reason. (Page 197.)
14. In lieu of our agreement, I will not bill you. (Page 215.)
15. For all intensive purposes, we have terminated our relationship with that vendor. (Page 212.)
16. I should have went earlier. (Verb Problems, pages 228, 229.)
17. I seen him with my own eyes. (Verb Problems, pages 228, 229.)
18. I done the work before I left the office. (Verb Problems, pages 228, 229.)
19. I had wrote him a letter. (Verb Problems, pages 228, 229.)
20. It don't work right. (Verb Problems, pages 228, 229.)

Answers to Twenty More Language Pet Peeves

1. Please give Bob and me an opportunity to bid on the project.
2. I felt bad for him.
3. Where's he?
4. The reason is we were late.
5. Because I am new here, I don't know the answer.
6. As we discussed, the credit has not yet been issued.
7. Our objectives are to purchase the new system by January 1, install it by March 1, and begin training the staff on March 15.

   or

   Our objectives are the following: to purchase the new system by January 1, install it by March 1, and begin training the staff on March 15.
8. There are many reasons why the strategy won't work.
9. We must discuss this further when we meet next week.
10. He's really well informed on that topic.
11. I spoke with Cindy in regard to the contract.
12. We've got fewer phone lines than we used to have.
13. I informed him about the reason.

    or, better

    I told him the reason.
14. In view of our agreement, I will not bill you.
15. For all intents and purposes, we have terminated our relationship with that vendor.
16. I should have gone earlier.
17. I saw him with my own eyes.
18. I did the work before I left the office.
19. I had written him a letter.
20. It doesn't work right.

Pronunciation Problems

Some words are frequently mispronounced. Say each word aloud or, better yet, tape yourself saying each word. Are you pronouncing the italicized letters in each word?

1. a*sk*ed (*ask'd,* NOT a*x*ed) To learn how to pronounce this correctly, say the word *task,* then drop the *t.* Now quickly add the *d.* (You'll feel your tongue touch your top front teeth as you do.)
2. in*t*eresting (NOT in*e*resting)
3. *h*uge (NOT *y*uge.)
4. *h*uman (NOT *y*uman.)
5. irre*lev*ant (NOT irre*ve*l*ant)
6. heigh*t* (NOT heig*th*)
7. reco*g*nize (NOT reconize)
8. lib*r*ary (NOT lib*a*ry)
9. stric*t*ly (NOT stric*k*ly)
10. gover*n*ment (NOT gove*r*ment)
11. hist*o*ry (NOT hist*r*y)
12. represen*ta*tive (NOT represen*tive*)
13. pi*c*ture (as in a painting) (NOT pitcher)
14. disas*t*rous (NOT dis-as-*ter*-ous)
15. mis*chievous* (MIS-che-vous, NOT mis-*CHEE-vi*-ous)
16. nu*clear* (noo-cle-er or nyoo-cle-er, NOT noo-*kyu*-ler)
17. in*tro*duce (NOT in*ner*-duce)
18. hun*d*red (NOT hun-*e*rd)
19. *sp*ecific (NOT *pa*-ci-fic)
20. tra*g*edy (NOT tra*de*gy)

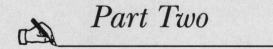

Part Two

Punctuation Points

3 The Comma, the Whole Comma, and Nothing but the Comma

I was working on a proof of one of my poems all morning, and took out a comma. In the afternoon I put it back.

—OSCAR WILDE

No punctuation mark causes more problems for more people more often than the comma. The reason Oscar Wilde and you and I find commas difficult is twofold. First, there are so many rules of commas use. In fact, there are more rules for comma use than for all the other punctuation marks combined. Second, there are many times when commas are simply a matter of personal preference. Thus, one writer puts a comma after a word because she wants the reader to pause (as I wanted you to after *thus*); another writer might eliminate it. These discretionary commas are used to add drama, to make a reader pause, or to help readers follow the ideas in a long sentence.

If you often find yourself in a state of comma trauma, relax. In this chapter we explain the dos and don'ts and the maybes. Some of the rules that follow are pretty straightforward, and these are presented first ("Straightforward": Rules 1–22); the ones that take more thought are presented second ("Complicated":

Rules 23–28); and the discretionary commas follow ("Discretionary": Rules 29–31). You will notice that some rules are followed by a note that says *Danger.* As you might expect, the *Danger* note points out errors that are frequently made in applying the rule at hand. Finally, the last section, "Commatose," explains other common errors.

Before the rules begin, though, why don't you test your comma capabilities by taking this Chapter Challenge?

Chapter Challenge

Each of the sentences below contains at least one comma error. The page numbers after each item tell you where the correct answer is explained. The answers are on page 59.

1. We spoke at length with Charlotte yet, we still did not get a complete explanation from her. (Rule 1, page 35.)
2. I would like to meet with Jim, and discuss the conference agenda. (Rule 1, Danger, page 36.)
3. I am delighted we had a chance to meet last week, I look forward to seeing you next month in Palm Springs. (Rule 32, page 55.)
4. Please put the dishes, plates and pots in the sink. (Rule 2, page 37.)
5. Yesterday I had a strange craving for a peanut butter and jelly sandwich. (Rule 6, page 40.)
6. After we concluded the deal we went to Burger King to celebrate. (Rule 9, page 41.)
7. Mike said, that he just realized that our mailing to 50,000 clients had the wrong price for every product. (Rule 34, page 56.)
8. Children, who cry in airplanes, are particularly unlovable. (Rule 27, page 50.)
9. The major presentation will be made by Fred, or Tom in the afternoon. (Rule 36, page 57.)

10. The symphony members are all retired, music teachers. (Rule 28, page 52.)
11. He lived in Altoona, Pennsylvania before moving to Pittsburgh. (Rule 13, page 44.)
12. The new president was Robert E. Krutcherfield, Jr. (Rule 16, page 44.)
13. I spoke to Arlen James, manager of information services about the errors on the report. (Rule 17, page 45.)
14. She had houses in all the best places including Rome, Paris, and New York. (Rule 26, page 50.)
15. We believe, that, your proposal, for the Megabuck Company campaign, is outrageous. (Rule 37, page 57.)

"No Price Too High"; "No, Price Too High"; and the Case of the Contested Will

Before the rules begin, I'd like to tell you two stories about misplaced or missing commas.

A woman went to Europe and decided to buy a fabulous necklace. She sent a telegram to her husband describing the piece and asking if the price was too high. He responded by fax: NO PRICE TOO HIGH. Delighted, she bought it. Only after he saw the necklace did he realize that he'd left out the comma after *no:* NO, PRICE TOO HIGH.

Commas can cause legal battles as well as simple misunderstandings. Several years ago, so the story goes, a person with a three-million-dollar estate wrote a will stating, "My estate is to be divided between Sarah, Rhonda and Kim." Sarah decided that her share should be $1.5 million. She based this on usage and punctuation issues. First, she said, the word *between* refers to two entities. Therefore, the three million should be divided in half. (Actually, she was wrong about this. If you want to know why, see "Troublesome Words and Phrases," page 200.) Second, she said, the lack of a comma between *Rhonda* and *Kim* clearly indicated that she formed one entity and Rhonda and Kim the other. Needless to say, Rhonda and Kim didn't see it that way, and a legal battle ensued to determine the intent of the deceased. In the end, after the judge found that the deceased's intent was to distribute the estate equally, the money was divided equally between the three sisters—minus attorneys' fees, of course.

Should you put a comma where you pause?

One of the questions people ask me is whether you should put a comma when you pause. The answer is, unfortunately, yes and no. Yes, put a comma after pauses, but no, not at every pause. Just major pauses. We pause frequently when we speak, and if we put a comma after every pause, we'll write sentences so full of bite-sized pieces that the reader will get annoyed.

Here, for example, is a sentence written by a comma-happy person, the one who remembers learning the guideline that you put commas where you pause:

> I think we should review the sales statistics, of the last quarter, before we meet in San Francisco. Our discussion should provide us with important ideas, and strategies, that could be implemented at the sales meeting, in August.

This, kind of, writing, is really, annoying.

The indented paragraph above should have no commas. Look how much clearer it is without the distracting commas:

> I think we should review the sales statistics of the last quarter before we meet in San Francisco. Our discussion should provide us with important ideas and strategies that could be implemented at the sales meeting in August.

Remember, one use of commas is to separate chunks, not bits, of information. Think about flutists. They take breaths at the end of a musical phrase, not after every couple of notes. Emulate them.

Where else do I need a comma?

Here are 37 rules of comma use, complete with dos, don'ts, and maybes, and plenty of examples of correct usage. The rules are divided into three categories: Straightforward, Complicated, and Discretionary. The items you will need most frequently are presented first within each category.

Straightforward

Commas That Glue Sentences Together

Rule 1. Use a comma before *and, but, or, yet, so, for,* and *nor* when these words are used to glue two complete sentences together. (Some authorities say the comma before *and* is optional.)

> *Correct:*
>> The committee met for four days, *and* it made some significant decisions.
>
>> *Sentence 1:* The committee met for four days
>
> + *Comma & Glue Word:* , *and*
>
> + *Sentence 2:* it made some significant progress.
>
>> You can't believe everything you hear, *but* it's fun to repeat it anyway. (Milton Berle)
>
>> *Sentence 1:* You can't believe everything you hear
>
> + *Comma & Glue Word:* , *but*
>
> + *Sentence 2:* it's fun to repeat it anyway.

DANGER: Do not place the comma after the words *and, but, or, yet, so, for,* or *nor.*

NOT: The committee met for four days and, it made some significant decisions.

BUT: The committee met for four days, and it made some significant decisions.

DANGER: Don't put a comma before *and* or the other words in Rule 1 unless there is a complete sentence after the glue word.

Incorrect:
> The committee met for four days, and made some significant decisions.

> *Sentence:* The committee met for four days

+ *Glue word: and*

+ *Not a Sentence:* made some significant decisions.

Correct:
> The committee met for four days and made some significant decisions.

Incorrect:
> I would like you to go with Linda to the game, or meet her there.

> *Sentence:* I would like you to go with Linda to the game

+ *Glue Word or*

+ *Not a Sentence:* meet her there.

Correct:
> I would like you to go with Linda to the game or meet her there.

Commas Between Items in a Series

Rule 2. When there are three or more items in a series, put a comma between the items. You may have learned that a comma is not needed before the *and*. Most authorities now agree that a comma before the *and* should be used to promote clarity.

Preferred:
> Please speak with Alice, Jim, Marta, or Fred before you proceed.

> There are three kinds of lies—lies, damned lies, and statistics. (Mark Twain)

Acceptable:
> Please speak with Alice, Jim, Marta or Fred before you proceed.

> There are three kinds of lies—lies, damned lies and statistics.

Note that the following sentences also contain a series of items and thus require commas between the items:

> He was asked to review the data, discuss the results with each unit head, and develop new procedures. (He was asked to take three actions.)

> She wanted to know how to do it, when to do it, and where to do it. (She wanted to know three things.)

> Some are born great, some achieve greatness, and some hire public relations officers. (Anthony Burgess)

Rule 3. When two short items are connected by *and* or *or*, do not use a comma.

> The Swedish flag is yellow and blue. (two colors)

> Call Bob or Jane for further information. (two people)

> She wanted to know how to do it and when to do it. (two things)

The manager was asked to review the data and discuss the results. (two actions)

I only know two tunes. One of them is "Yankee Doodle" and the other isn't. (Ulysses S. Grant)

However, if the first item is long, use a comma for clarity.

A bit confusing:

His dream was to complete his studies in sales and marketing and get his first job.

Clear:

His dream was to complete his studies in sales and marketing, and get his first job.

A bit confusing:

The vice president met with Mr. John Sage to discuss the latest developments in the complicated negotiation with the subcontractor and to get his ideas on the Smithson case.

Clear:

The vice president met with Mr. John Sage to discuss the latest developments in the complicated negotiation with the subcontractor, and to get his ideas on the Smithson case.

☞ **NOTE:** When one long item and one short item are joined by *and,* put the short item first for improved clarity. You will then most likely not need a comma.

Clearer yet:

The vice president met with Mr. John Sage to get his ideas on the Smithson case and to discuss the latest developments in the complicated negotiation with the subcontractor.

Commas with Introductory Material

Rules 4–9 explain how commas are used to set off introductory material from the main sentence. Introductory material, as you will see in a moment, can consist of one word or many words. Here are six examples of introductory material in front of one of the simplest and most important sentences in English (or any language): *I love you.*

> *Truly,* I love you.
>
> *Of course,* I love you.
>
> *With all my heart,* I love you.
>
> *Every once in a while,* I love you.
>
> *Because you are completely devoid of common sense,* I love you.
>
> *Whenever I think of the pot roast you made last Tuesday,* I love you.

Introductory material can tell you how much (*truly* or *with all my heart*) or why (*because you are completely devoid of common sense*) or when (*every once in a while, whenever I think of the pot roast*). It can also make a casual comment like *of course.* It can consist of a word, a phrase, or a clause. But in each case, the material is merely introductory; it simply leads us to main sentence: *I love you.*

Here are the six rules for commas with different kinds of introductory material.

Commas with Transitional and Comment Words

Rule 4. Put a comma after transitional words like *first* and *therefore* and *for instance* when these words introduce a sentence. They are called transitional words because they help move the reader to a new idea.

> I believe in reincarnation. I've had other lives. I know. I've had clues. First of all, I'm exhausted. (Carol Siskind)

Therefore, we are not able to make a commitment at this time.

I happen to be the suspicious type. For instance, I've always felt that reincarnation is just a sneaky way to sell more tombstones. (Robert Orben)

Other common transitional words are *also, in addition, in summary, however, for example,* and *as a result.*

Rule 5. Put a comma after words like *obviously* and *of course* when these words make a comment about the sentence.

Obviously, someone had given the manager misinformation.

Of course, Jane knew the answer.

Other comment words are *in my opinion, clearly, certainly, unfortunately, undoubtedly,* and *in fact.*

Rule 6. Put commas after introductory words that tell *when.* These commas are not required, but they are permissible.

Recently, we discussed the agenda for the meeting in Chicago.

Occasionally, we revise the employment criteria.

In the future, everyone will be famous for fifteen minutes. (Andy Warhol)

Other *when* words are *frequently, yesterday, last week, often, tomorrow, after, before,* and *during.*

Commas after Short and Long Prepositional Phrases

Rule 7. A comma is optional after a short prepositional phrase, but required after a long one. Consider phrases with five or more syllables as long.

At the meeting (*or* At the meeting,) we decided to cancel the project.

At the meeting in the ballroom of the Waldorf-Astoria, we decided to cancel the project.

During his talk (*or* During his talk,) Roger made a number of brilliant points.

During his talk to our chemical engineers, Roger made a number of brilliant points.

Commas after Introductory Phrases with Dates

Rule 8. Put a comma after an introductory phrase that contains a date. The commas are mandatory if all three elements of the date are given and optional if only two elements of the date are given.

On June 1, 1994, I saw Elvis Presley in a car wash.

On June 2 (*or* On June 2,) we started dating.

In 1995 (*or* In 1995,) I told Elvis to stop calling me.

On Tuesday (*or* On Tuesday,) Elvis and I got back together.

Commas with Cliff-Hangers

Rule 9. Use a comma between a "cliff-hanger" clause and the rest of the sentence. A cliff-hanger clause is an introductory group of words containing a subject and a verb. They are called cliff-hangers because they leave you hanging until you get to the end of the sentence. Cliff-hangers often start with these words: *after, although, as, because, before, if, since, unless, when,* and *while.**

---

* See *Cliff-hanger* in the Glossary for a complete list of cliff-hanger words.

In each of the following sentences, the cliff-hanger clause is followed by a comma and ends with a complete sentence.

> When Sears comes out with a riding vacuum cleaner, then I'll clean the house. (Roseanne Barr)
>
> *Cliff-hanger:* When Sears comes out with a riding vacuum cleaner,
>
> *Complete Sentence:* then I'll clean the house.
>
> From the moment I picked your book up until I laid it down, I was convulsed with laughter. Someday I intend to read it. (Groucho Marx)
>
> *Cliff-hanger:* From the moment I picked your book up until I laid it down,
>
> *Complete Sentence:* I was convulsed with laughter.
>
> If my doctor told me I only had six minutes to live, I wouldn't brood. I'd type a little faster. (Isaac Asimov)
>
> *Cliff-hanger:* If my doctor told me I only had six minutes to live,
>
> *Complete Sentence:* I wouldn't brood.

DANGER: Don't use a comma when the cliff-hanger clause comes at the end of the sentence unless the cliff-hanger clause is clearly an afterthought.

No comma needed:
> Ms. Jones took action after I found the $25,000 error.

No comma needed:
> Sue will call you when she returns from vacation.

Comma needed because material is an afterthought:
> Sue will call you when she returns from vacation, after she's had time to read her mail.

A dash could also be used before the afterthought.

Commas with Or

Rule 10. Use commas to set aside a definition or explanatory note after the word *or*.

> Accrued interest, or interest that has been earned but not paid, must be added to the financial report.

For other comma uses with *or,* see Rule 2, page 37, and Rule 36, page 57.

Commas with Dates

Rule 11. Use commas between items in a date when the month, day, and year *or* the weekday and date are given.

> The United States gained its independence on July 4, 1776.

> I will see you Wednesday, August 20, in the conference room.

Rule 12. No comma is needed between the month and year if just those two elements of the date are given.

> The new computer system was installed in February 1991.

✍ **NOTE** about *st, th, rd,* and *nd:* Don't use these when the month is given.

Incorrect:
> I look forward to seeing you February 10th.

Correct:
> I look forward to seeing you February 10.

Correct:
> I look forward to seeing you on the 10th.

Commas with Cities and States

Rule 13. When city and state are given, put a comma after city and state.

She has lived in Omaha, Nebraska, for the past ten years.

(When there is a list of cities and states, see Rule 3, page 65.)

Commas with Direct Quotations

Rule 14. Use a comma before a direct quote.

He said, "I just mailed you the check."

Exception: If the quotation is very short and is woven into the sentence, the comma is not necessary.

She said "Okay" and just kept walking.

If the quotation is several sentences long, use a colon. (See Rule 8, page 70.)

Rule 15. Use commas when the word *too* (meaning *also*) appears within a sentence. Omit the comma if it appears at the end.

You, too, must be aware of this.

I think the timing of the offer is important too.

Commas with Jr. and Numbers

Rule 16. Use a comma before and after *Jr.* and *III* in last names only if the individual does.

Martin Luther King, *Jr.,* was awarded the Nobel Peace Prize.

Some people whose names include a *Jr.* (John Smith Jr.) or number (John Smith III) don't use a comma to separate their name and its descriptor. Some do. When in doubt, ask. It's important to get names right.

Commas with Professional and Job Titles

Rule 17. Set aside professional titles and job titles that follow the person's name with commas. (Don't forget the second comma.)

My husband, Martin J. Feierman, *M.D.*, would like to play center field for the New York Mets.

Ron Pitielli, *manager of consumer affairs,* is on a special assignment.

Barbara Stedman, *the mediation lawyer,* is the only person who can resolve this case.

For information about capitalizing job titles see Rules 2, 3, 4, pages 109–110.

DANGER: Be sure to use two commas—not one—to set aside additional material or job titles.

Incorrect:
I am referring your request for the recipe for Hashish Brownies to Alice B. Toklas, Ms. Stein's secretary for response.

Correct:
I am referring your request for the recipe for Hashish Brownies to Alice B. Toklas, Ms. Stein's secretary, for response.

Commas with Company Names

Rule 18. Check a company's stationery or ask the operator if the company uses a comma before *Inc.* or *Ltd.* Some do; others don't.

> McGraw-Hill, Inc.
>
> Smith Barney Inc.

Commas with Parenthetical Expressions

Rule 19. Set aside parenthetical expressions (side comments) that interrupt the sentence flow with a pair of commas.

> You know, of course, that I'm only joking.
>
> Bob feels, and I agree with him, that we must make a decision now.
>
> My cat, believe it or not, has decided that our velvet couch is a scratching post.

Dashes or parentheses could have been used in place of the commas in each example.

Commas with However, Therefore, *and* Nevertheless *When They Interrupt the Flow of a Sentence*

Rule 20. Set aside the words *however, therefore, nevertheless,* and similar words with commas when these words interrupt the flow of a sentence.

> We agreed, however, that there was no need to take immediate action.
>
> The committee, therefore, postponed making a decision.

DANGER: If *however, therefore,* or *nevertheless* glue together two sentences, rather than interrupt one, a semicolon is needed. (See Rule 1, page 63.)

Commas with the Words Yes, No, and Well

Rule 21. Use commas to set aside the words *yes, no,* and *well*.

> Yes, I can send the package immediately.
>
> I know that, yes, he will contact the client.
>
> Eternal rest sounds comforting in the pulpit. Well, you try it once and see how heavy time will hang on your hands. (Mark Twain)

Commas with Names of People Being Addressed

Rule 22. Use a comma when addressing a person.

> Mr. Smith, you could be the lucky winner of $100,000 in prizes.
>
> We suggest, Mr. Smith, that you mail in your coupon today.

Complicated

Commas with Namely, For Example, I.E., That Is, and E.G.

How the expressions *namely, for example, i.e., that is,* and *e.g.* are handled depends on whether these expressions introduce words or phrases that end a sentence or come within a sentence. Rules 23 and 24 explain the different types of punctuation and offer some suggestions for clarity.

Rule 23. Commas precede and follow the expressions *namely, for example, i.e., that is,* **and** *e.g.* **when these words introduce a series of items at the end of a sentence.**

> She has three hobbies, *namely,* swimming, running, and skydiving.

> We offered to accommodate the customer several ways, for example, by reducing the price, adding bonus items, and eliminating all delivery fees.

Other options: There are several other acceptable ways to punctuate sentences that include the words *namely, for example, i.e., that is,* and *e.g.*

> She has several hobbies; namely, swimming, running, and skydiving.

> She has several hobbies: namely, swimming, running, and skydiving.

> She has several hobbies—namely, swimming, running, and skydiving.

> She has several hobbies (namely, swimming, running, and skydiving).

🖎 **NOTE:** Sentences like those above will be clearer and more graceful if you delete the expressions *namely, for example, i.e., that is,* and *e.g.* and use a colon instead.

> She has three hobbies: swimming, running, and skydiving.

> We offered to accommodate the customer several ways: by reducing the price, adding bonus items, and eliminating all delivery fees.

Rule 24. If the expressions *namely, for example, i.e., that is,* **and** *e.g.* **occur within a sentence, use commas, dashes, or parentheses as follows:**

Acceptable:

Several of the tools, namely, the wrench and the screw-driver, are finely made.

Preferred:

Several of the tools—namely, the wrench and the screwdriver—are finely made.

Several of the tools (namely, the wrench and the screw-driver) are finely made.

☞ **NOTE:** Use dashes or parentheses, rather than commas, when the phrase after *namely* contains commas within it.

Confusing:

The consultant sent us so much unnecessary material, namely, articles, tapes, testimonials, books, and bro-chures, that we threw most of it out.

Clear:

The consultant sent us so much unnecessary material—namely, articles, tapes, testimonials, books, and bro-chures—that we threw most of it out.

The consultant sent us so much unnecessary material (namely, articles, tapes, testimonials, books, and bro-chures) that we threw most of it out.

Rule 25. If *for example* ends the sentence, use a comma.

One book contained over 1,000 pages, for example.

DANGER: *I.e.* and *e.g.* do not mean the same thing. *I.e.* is the Latin abbreviation for *that is* and *e.g.* is an abbreviation for *for example.*

Which millionaire is giving away more treasure?

The one who says:

> I want you to have everything I own, i.e., my Rolls-Royce.

or the one who says:

> I want you to have everything I own, e.g., my Rolls-Royce.

The second, of course—the first person is giving you *only* the Rolls-Royce. The second is providing many things. The Rolls-Royce is just one example of luxuries to come.

Commas with Such As *and* Including

Rule 26. Use commas before *such as* and *including*.

> He is interested in several companies, *such as* IBM, General Foods, and International Paper.

> She had worked in many big cities, *including* New York, Chicago, and Los Angeles, before she moved to a farm in Nebraska.

DANGER: Do not put anything—no commas, no colons—after *such as* and *including*.

Commas with Additional Information

Rule 27. If you name something and immediately provide <u>additional</u> information about it, you must set the additional information aside in a pair of commas. If you name something and then add <u>essential</u> information about it, do not set the information aside in a pair of commas.

As you read the examples of additional and essential information that follow, note that each of the sentences under *additional information* can be read without the material in the commas and still deliver an accurate restatement of the sentence *King Lear scares me every time I see it.*

Examples of additional information (commas needed):
> *King Lear,* the Shakespearian play, scares me every time I see it.

> *King Lear,* which I read in my sophomore year in college, scares me every time I see it.

In the examples of essential information that follow, the information after *King Lear* cannot be deleted without radically changing the meaning of each sentence.

Examples of essential information (no commas needed):
> The *King Lear* that I saw on television last night didn't scare me.

> The *King Lear* that I helped produce in my sophomore year hardly scared me.

If we remove *that I saw on television last night* from the first sentence, we are left with *the* King Lear *didn't scare me.* That's not what the sentence means: It's *the* King Lear *that I saw on television last night* that didn't scare me. That phrase is essential to the meaning of the sentence and thus cannot be set aside in commas.

Similarly, if we remove *that I helped produce in my sophomore year* from the second sentence, we are left with *the* King Lear *hardly scared me.* Again, this is not an accurate restatement of the sentence: It's *the* King Lear *that I helped produce in my sophomore year* that hardly scared me.

More Examples

Additional information:
> I know Linda Stefanski, the woman who won the lottery twice.

The point of the sentence is that *I know Linda Stefanski*; the information about her winning the lottery twice is simply additional.

Essential information:
> I know a woman who won the lottery twice.

The point of the sentence is that *I know a woman who won the lottery twice,* not that *I know a woman.*

Additional information:
My boss, who never abuses his staff members, is an angel.

My boss is an angel is the main idea of the sentence. The *who never abuses his staff members* is additional information and should be set aside in commas.

Essential information:
Bosses who abuse their staff members should be sentenced to bosses' prison.

Not every boss should be sentenced to bosses' prison; only those who abuse their staff members. Therefore *who abuse their staff members* is essential to our understanding of the sentence and should not be set aside in commas.

✍ **NOTE:** To tell whether a word, phrase, or clause is essential or merely additional, read the sentence without that material and determine whether the meaning of the sentence has changed significantly. If it has, no commas are needed. If it hasn't, commas are needed.

Commas to Separate Adjectives

Rule 28. When two or more adjectives precede a noun and each one independently describes the noun, put a comma between the adjectives. If they do not, omit the comma.

To determine whether each word independently describes the noun, restate the sentence in the way demonstrated below. (As you will see, you will have to add words like *who is* or *that is* to the sentence.) If the new sentence reads smoothly and makes sense, a comma is needed in the original sentence. If it does not, no comma should be used.

Original sentence:
Rachel is a talented, careful photographer.

Restated sentence:
Rachel is a photographer who is talented and careful flows well. Therefore, the comma is needed.

Original sentence:
We feared the lawyer was leading us into a lengthy, expensive case.

Restated sentence:
We feared the lawyer was leading us into a case that would be lengthy and expensive flows. Therefore, the comma is needed.

Original sentence:
It usually takes more than three weeks to prepare a good impromptu speech. (Mark Twain)

Restated sentence:
It usually takes more than three weeks to prepare a speech that is good and impromptu does not flow smoothly. Therefore, no comma is needed. In this sentence, *impromptu speech* is considered one entity, and the single adjective *good* describes it. No comma is needed, of course, between one adjective and the word it describes.

Original sentence:
Please take advantage of this new introductory offer.

Restated sentence:
Please take advantage of this offer that is new and introductory doesn't flow. In this sentence *introductory offer* is considered one unit; *new* describes it. No comma is needed.

🖎 **NOTE:** Adjectives of number and color and the words *old* and *young* generally do not require commas.

---

the glamorous gold slippers

the four broken glasses

the charming young man

the little old man

Discretionary

Rule 29. Always use a comma for clarity's sake.

Although both sentences below have only short prepositional phrases and thus, strictly speaking, do not require commas, commas must be added to guide the reader.

Confusing:
> In conflict people experience specific physiological changes.

Clear:
> In conflict, people experience specific physiological changes.

Confusing:
> To Frank Robert was a person of endless fascination.

Clear:
> To Frank, Robert was a person of endless fascination.

Commas for Drama

Rule 30. Use a comma to create special emphasis or drama.

> He was sneaky, very sneaky.

> I hate music, especially when it's played. (Jimmy Durante)

A dash can be used for even more drama.

> I had a very favorable impression of him—at first.

Rule 31. Put a comma after sentences that begin with *then, thus,* **or** *hence* **if you want to place special emphasis on the introductory word; do not put a comma if no special emphasis is desired.**

> First, put all the papers in the file cabinet next to the window. Then, take them all out again!

> Let's wait until Jim returns. Then we'll have a better idea of how to proceed.

Comma-tose (How to Avoid Common Comma Errors)

Rule 32. Do not put a comma between two sentences. Only a period or a semicolon can be used. The one exception is noted below.

Incorrect:
> I look forward to meeting you next Tuesday, I hope you can come.

Correct:
> I look forward to meeting you next Tuesday. I hope you can come.

or

> I look forward to meeting you next Tuesday; I hope you can come.

Exception: You may use a comma to make one sentence out of two or more if, and only if, the sentences are very short.

Correct:
> He came. He saw. He conquered.

> He came, he saw, he conquered.

Rule 33. Do not put a comma between the last adjective and the noun it describes.

Incorrect:

The vice president described Alex as a brilliant, dedi-cated, hardworking, man.

Correct:

The vice president described Alex as a brilliant, dedi-cated, hardworking man.

After all, if the sentence had been *The vice president described Alex as a hardworking man,* you would not have written *The vice president described Alex as a hardworking, man.* There is no reason to put a comma there when other descriptive words are present before the word *man.*

Rule 34. Don't use a comma when paraphrasing, that is, when you communicate what a person said without quoting the exact words spoken. (The *that* in the sentences below is optional.)

Incorrect:

He said, that the check was in the mail.

He said, the check was in the mail.

Correct:

He said that the check was in the mail.

He said the check was in the mail.

Rule 35. Do not put a comma after the word *that* before a direct quotation.

Incorrect:

She said that, "We will not implement the project as directed."

Correct:

She said that "we will not implement the project as directed." (Do not capitalize the first word of a quoted sentence if you have incorporated the quoted sentence into your own sentence.)

or

> She said, "We will not implement the project as directed."

Rule 36. Do not use one comma with *or* when listing options. Use either two commas or none.

Incorrect:

> Call Bob, or Jane for directions.

Correct:

> Call Bob or Jane for directions. (This means to call either one; it does not matter which person you call.)

Possibly Correct:

> Call Bob, or Jane, for directions. (This means that the person to call is Bob. Jane, because she is set aside with commas, is presented as an alternative of lesser importance.)

Rule 37. Do not place a comma every time you pause. None of the commas in the incorrect version are justified by any of the rules of comma use.

Incorrect:

> The reason, for his decision, was that the vendor had not complied with the terms, of the contract.

Correct:

> The reason for his decision was that the vendor had not complied with the terms of the contract.

One Final Note on Commas

Whether or not to use a given comma requires common sense as well as knowledge of the rules. As you debate whether or not a comma is needed, consider the whole sentence and the thought that you are trying to express, rather than an individual phrase or clause. After all, the most important goal of writing is clarity, so be sure that each comma you add makes it easier, and not harder, for your reader to follow your thoughts.

To make this point clear, I've written several sentences in two styles. In the first one I've put in every possible comma and indicated the rules that could be used to justify each comma. In the second, I've used only those commas that make the writing clear and graceful.

Original:

The letter, which, in part, criticized our financial controls, is, on the whole, complimentary.

Reason for the comma after *letter* and after *controls*, Rule 7. Reason for the commas that set aside *in part* and *on the whole*, Rule 19.

Revised:

The letter, which in part criticized our financial controls, is on the whole complimentary.

The author's meaning is clearer when only the one set of commas is used.

Original:

Are you attending the meeting on Friday, and, if you are, could you provide the sandwiches?

Reason for the comma after *Friday*, Rule 1. Reason for the comma after *if you are*, Rule 9.

Revised:

Are you attending the meeting on Friday, and if you are, could you provide the sandwiches?

Two commas result in a smoother reading.

Similarly:

Original:

I can't believe that, if you had gone with me, we both would have met Robert Redford!

Revised:
> I can't believe that if you had gone with me, we both would have met Robert Redford!

Answers to Chapter Challenge

1. We spoke at length with Charlotte, yet we still did not get a complete explanation from her.
2. I would like to meet with Jim and discuss the conference agenda.
3. I am delighted we had a chance to meet last week. I look forward to seeing you next month in Palm Springs.

   or

   I am delighted we had a chance to meet last week; I look forward to seeing you next month in Palm Springs.
4. Actually, this one is not incorrect; however, I wanted to alert you to the preferred punctuation: Please put the dishes, plates, and pots in the sink.
5. This is correct as it stands. I just wanted you to know that you *could* have a comma after *Yesterday.*
6. After we concluded the deal, we went to Burger King to celebrate.
7. Mike said that he just realized that our mailing to 50,000 clients had the wrong price for every product.
8. Children who cry in airplanes are particularly unlovable.
9. The major presentation will be made by Fred or Tom in the afternoon.
10. The symphony members are all retired music teachers. (Remember, the orchestra members are not teachers who are retired and music. Rather, they are music teachers who are retired.)
11. He lived in Altoona, Pennsylvania, before moving to Pittsburgh.

12. The new president was Robert E. Krutcherfield Jr. (Most people do not place a comma before the *Jr.*)
13. I spoke to Arlen James, manager of information services, about the errors on the report.
14. She had houses in all the best places, including Rome, Paris, and New York.
15. We believe that your proposal for the Megabuck Company campaign is outrageous. (No commas needed.)

4 More Punctuation
Semicolons, Colons, Quotation Marks, and Apostrophes

> Writing is easy; all you do is sit staring at a blank sheet of paper until the drops of blood form on your forehead.
>
> —GENE FOWLER

This chapter explains how semicolons and colons are different, when to use quotation marks (and when not to), and why the word pair *its/it's* causes so much confusion.

Chapter Challenge

Each sentence contains an error in semicolons, colons, quotation marks, or apostrophes. The page number after each item tells you where the answer is explained. The answers are on pages 78, 79.

1. We had planned to drive to the conference together, however, we later decided to travel separately. (Rule 1, page 63.)

2. We entered the room on tiptoe, the baby was sleeping. (Rule 2, page 64.)
3. The conferences will take place in Rabat, Morocco, Tokyo, Japan, and Siena, Italy. (Rule 3, page 65.)
4. Dear Mr. Clark; (Rule 4, page 66.)
5. He had three items on the agenda;

   1. Explaining the results of the tests
   2. Announcing the new procedures
   3. Getting his bosses' agreement to fund the project (Rule 5, page 67.)

6. Within a single hour, the puppy had wreaked the following devastation; chewed the electric cord, pulled the tablecloth off the table, and eaten my son's pet gerbil. (Rule 6, page 68.)
7. Always keep in mind: haste makes waste. (Rule 7, page 70.)
8. He described himself as "just a country boy". (Rules 9, 10, page 72.)
9. I thought I heard him say, "Are you trying to intimidate me"? (Rule 12, page 72.)
10. I tried to read Getting onto the Information Superhighway in *Business Week*, but I fell asleep at the wheel. (Rule 14, page 73.)
11. One witness' testimony was so weak that we anticipated an acquittal. (Rule 17, page 74.)
12. Its difficult to put the chart in it's proper place when the file room is locked except for two hours each day. (Rule 21, page 76.)
13. Please bring "only" one friend to the party. (Rule 15, Danger, page 73.)
14. This music should be played molto adagio, or very slowly. (Rule 15, page 73.)
15. Mr. Jones' secretary functions as a corporate guard dog. (Rule 18, page 75.)

Semicolons

Semicolons represent a pause that's longer than a comma but shorter than a period (or full stop, as the English call it). If periods are a red light, and commas are a yellow, a semicolon is a red *and* a yellow. It means stop, but not for long.

Some people claim that the semicolon is an endangered mark of punctuation—soon to be extinct. I hope not. I agree with Abraham Lincoln, who said, "With educated people, I suppose, punctuation is a matter of rule; with me it is a matter of feeling. But I must say I have a great respect for the semicolon; it's a useful little chap."

Semicolons have three main uses, as illustrated in the following three rules.

Rule 1. Use a semicolon before and a comma after any of the following words when they are used to glue two sentences together: *however, therefore, consequently, for example, furthermore, nevertheless, accordingly, otherwise, moreover, on the contrary, for instance, that is, besides, instead, hence,* thus.**

Incorrect:

Jack had a good work record, however, he had trouble finding a job.

Correct:

Jack had a good work record; however, he had trouble finding a job.

Incorrect:

We want the presentation to be flawless, therefore we will rehearse it many times.

---

* You don't have to have a comma after *hence* and *thus,* and some authorities say that, if there is no major pause after any of the words in this list, the comma may be deleted.

Correct:

> We want the presentation to be flawless; therefore, we will rehearse it many times.

Incorrect:

> They had made several efforts to notify the panel members, for example, they left messages on voice mail and sent a fax to each person.

Correct:

> They made several efforts to notify the panel members; for example, they left messages on voice mail and sent a fax to each person.

Incorrect:

> The division was not profitable last year, hence the company may sell it.

Correct:

> The division was not profitable last year; hence the company may sell it.

Each of these four sentences could have been written as two separate sentences:

> Jack had a good work record. However, he had trouble finding a job.

> We want the presentation to be flawless. Therefore, we will rehearse it many times.

> They made several efforts to notify the panel members. For example, they left messages on voice mail and sent a fax to each person.

> The division was not profitable last year. Hence the company may sell it.

Rule 2. Use semicolons to glue two closely related sentences together if there is no word gluing the two sentences together.

Never lend books, for no one ever returns them; the only books I have in my library are books that other folks have lent me. (Anatole France)

When a man wants to murder a tiger he calls it sport; when a tiger wants to murder him he calls it ferocity. (George Bernard Shaw)

Rule 3. Use a semicolon to separate items in a series if any of the items have commas in them. In other words, semicolons are used as "supercommas" to separate items in a series.

Incorrect:

She lived in Portland, Oregon, Houston, Texas, Buffalo, New York, and three other cities.

Preferred:

She lived in Portland, Oregon; Houston, Texas; Buffalo, New York; and three other cities.

Acceptable:

She lived in Portland, Oregon; Houston, Texas; Buffalo, New York, and three other cities.

Preferred:

Marcia Tannenbaum, director of human resources; Miles Johnson, director of finance; and Bob Rosen, director of marketing, attended the meeting.

Acceptable:

Marcia Tannenbaum, director of human resources, Miles Johnson, director of finance, and Bob Rosen, director of marketing, attended the meeting.

Colons

Colons always announce something: They say, here's the letter, here's the list, here's what I mean. Think of them as the sound of trumpets before an important announcement.

Rule 4. Use a colon after the Dear So-and-So of each business letter. A comma or a colon can be used if the writer is on a first-name basis with the reader.

Correct:
Dear Mr. Clark:

Acceptable if you are on a first-name basis with the reader:
Dear Robert:

or

Dear Robert,

DANGER: Do not use a semicolon after the Dear So-and-So.

Incorrect:
Dear Mr. Clark;

Dear Robert;

You'll find more on salutations in Chapter 14, Answers to Your Questions on Letter Writing, on page 177.)

Colons Before Vertical and Horizontal Lists

The next two rules explain the use of colons before two kinds of lists, vertical and horizontal. A vertical list looks like this:

Please bring the following with you:

• Pens
• Paper
• Laptops

A horizontal list looks like this:

Please bring the following with you: pens, papers, and laptops.

Rule 5. Use a colon before items in a vertical list.

She wanted three things:

1. A good job
2. A nice home
3. A million dollars

She wanted to:

1. Land a good job
2. Have a nice home
3. Inherit a million dollars

She wanted:

1. To land a good job
2. To have a nice home
3. To inherit a million dollars

Question: What is the correct mark of punctuation to put at the end of each item in the list?

That is a good question. Unfortunately, the authorities don't agree on the answer except in this respect: If each item is a sentence, a period is required after each sentence. (But you could have guessed that anyway.)

Here are the options when the items do not form complete sentences.

Option 1—Nothing after each item

Three problems prevented us from completing the project:

1. Lack of supervision
2. Insufficient funds
3. Improper staffing levels

Option 2—A period after each item

Three problems prevented us from completing the project:

1. Lack of supervision.
2. Insufficient funds.
3. Improper staffing levels.

Option 3—Two commas, one period

Three problems prevented us from completing the project:

1. Lack of supervision,
2. Insufficient funds, and
3. Improper staffing levels.

Option 4—Two semicolons, one period (the style preferred in legal writing)

Three problems prevented us from completing the project:

1. Lack of supervision;
2. Insufficient funds; and
3. Improper staffing levels.

Rule 6. Use colons to introduce a horizontal list after a noun or a complete thought that could stand alone as a sentence.

There are two modes of transport in Los Angeles: car and ambulance. (Fran Lebowitz, *Social Studies*)

DANGER: Do not place a colon after these words: *to, with, on, by,* or *includes* in a horizontal list. Remember, in a horizontal list a colon can follow only a noun or a complete thought that could stand alone.

Incorrect:

Her objectives were to: land a good job, have a nice home, and inherit a million dollars.

Her objectives were: to land a good job, have a nice home, and inherit a million dollars.

Correct:

She had three objectives: to land a good job, have a nice home, and inherit a million dollars. (Colon comes after a sentence.)

☜ **NOTE:** The two incorrect sentences above and on page 68 would be correct if the colon in each sentence were removed.

Her objectives were the following: to land a good job, to have a nice home, and to inherit a million dollars. (*The following*, a noun, can be added. Although the sentence is now grammatically correct, it is cumbersome. Avoid using *the following*, if possible.)

DANGER: Do not use a semicolon to introduce a horizontal list.

Incorrect:

She gave three reasons for being late on Sunday; heavy traffic, a broken watch, and a party on Saturday night.

Correct:

She gave three reasons for being late on Sunday: heavy traffic, a broken watch, and a party on Saturday night.

☜ **NOTE:** Colons can replace the expressions *namely, i.e.,* and *that is.* Sentences are more graceful when this is done.

Acceptable:

> She was interested in several careers, namely, fashion, journalism, and public relations.

Preferred:

> She was interested in several careers: fashion, journalism, and public relations.

Rule 7. Colons can also be used like semicolons between two closely related thoughts when the second thought explains the first.

> Santa Claus has the right idea: visit people once a year. (Victor Borge)

If the first thought introduces a rule or principle, capitalize the first word of the second thought.

> She made this clear: No one was going on any business trips this quarter.

Rule 8. A colon rather than a comma may be used to introduce a quotation consisting of more than one sentence. Note that the quotation marks are placed only at the beginning and the end of the entire quotation.

> The policy manual states: "Employees must show their name tags to security personnel as they enter the building. Any visitor, vendor, or person acting on behalf of a vendor must complete the sign-in sheet and receive a visitor's identification badge."

If the quoted material will occupy more than four or five lines of text, use this preferred method: (1) indent the quoted material five spaces from each text margin, (2) leave a blank line above and below the quotation, and (3) do not put quotation marks around the quoted material (the indentation takes the place of the quotation marks).

The policy manual states:

> Employees must show their name tags to security personnel as they enter the building. Any visitor, vendor, or person acting on behalf of a vendor must complete the sign-in sheet and receive a visitor's identification badge. This badge must be visible on the person visiting the building.

🖎 **NOTE:** Colons can prevent ambiguity.

Unclear:

> Two things affect productivity, pay and work environment.

Does the author mean that (*a*) pay and work environment affect productivity? Or that (*b*) two things affect productivity, pay, and work environment? Note how the meaning changes with the addition of a colon or a comma.

Clear:

> (*a*) Two things affect productivity: pay and work environment.

> (*b*) Two things affect productivity, pay, and work environment.

A dash could also be used in place of the colon.

> Two things affect productivity—pay and work environment.

Quotation Marks

When we think of quotation marks, we think of their use to indicate someone's exact words. However, quotation marks have two other functions as well, as you will see in Rules 14 and 15.

Rule 9. Use quotation marks around *someone's exact words* whether written or spoken.

> Rita Rudner said, "My boyfriend and I broke up. He wanted to get married, and I didn't want him to."

> I get no respect. I get mail that starts, "You may already be a loser." (Rodney Dangerfield)

Rule 10. In the United States, periods and commas always go inside the quotation marks whether the quoted material is a sentence, a group of words, or a single word. (This may not be logical, but it's the rule. The rest of the English-speaking world does not follow the American practice.)

Each of the following is correct:

> I asked my doctor what to do for a sprained ankle. He said, "Limp." (Milton Berle)

> Want to have some fun? Send someone a telegram and on the top put "page two." (Henny Youngman)

> I live in a rough neighborhood. We just put up a sign. It says, "Drive Fast. The life you save may be your own." (Rodney Dangerfield)

Exception: In the United States, lawyers do not follow this rule.

Rule 11. Place semicolons and colons outside the quotation marks.

> The client said, "The check is in the mail"; however, it wasn't.

> Please bring me the two letters marked "Rush": the one for Mr. Wickers and the one for Ms. Farley.

Rule 12. Place question marks inside the quotation mark in every case except one: when a sentence begins with a question and is followed by a quoted statement, phrase, or word. Study the examples that follow.

Inside:

I have poor eyesight. When I take an eye test, the doctor points to the letters and he calls them out and says, "True or false?" (Woody Allen) (Starts with a statement and is followed by a quoted question.)

Did Jane ask, "Is this the final draft?" (Starts with a question but is followed by a quoted question.)

Outside:

Did Jane say, "This is the final draft"? (Starts with a question and is followed by a quoted statement.)

Rule 13. Treat exclamation points in exactly the same way as question marks.

How dare he refer to his assistant as "Mr. Pea Brain"!

Rule 14. Use quotation marks around titles of articles in magazines and chapters in books. (The name of the book or magazine is either italicized or underscored.)

His article "New Directions in Marketing" was accepted for publication in *Business Week.*

Rule 15. Use quotation marks around slang words, technical terms, or words that are used in an unusual way. (Italics and underscoring can also be used for this purpose.)

Bart Simpson says he is a "radical dude."

"Bioremediation" is the use of microorganisms to degrade and eliminate contaminants from the soil or groundwater.

The homeless man's "castle" was a cardboard box.

DANGER: Do not use quotation marks to emphasize words. Instead use italics, underlining, or boldface type.

Incorrect:
The meeting will begin at "exactly" 4:30 P.M.

Correct:
The meeting will begin at *exactly* 4:30 P.M.

The meeting will begin at **exactly** 4:30 P.M.

The meeting will begin at exactly 4:30 P.M.

Rule 16. Use single quotation marks to enclose a quotation within a quotation.

Faith explained, "The instructor said, 'No class will be held next Tuesday.' "

Apostrophes

When we think of apostrophes, we think of possession, but apostrophes do more than that. That's why we've divided this section into three parts:

Apostrophes Indicating Possession

Apostrophes Indicating Contractions

Apostrophes Indicating Plurals

Apostrophes Indicating Possession

Rule 17. To make singular words possessive, add apostrophe and *s. This rule applies even if the word ends in* s. (Note the one exception in Rule 18.)

one witness's testimony

one actress's role

one day's testimony

one lawyer's office

one man's dream

one child's toy

Rule 18. If a singular proper name ends in *s*, some authorities recommend using apostrophe and *s*. Others state that if doing so would make the name extremely difficult to pronounce, just add the apostrophe.

Acceptable:

Moses's farewell speech

Moses' farewell speech

Bill Gates's millions

Bill Gates' millions

Both *The New York Times* and *The Wall Street Journal* use apostrophe and *s* for names ending in *s*, which seems to be the most common practice.

Rule 19. To make plural words possessive:
Add an apostrophe if the word ends in *s*.

two witnesses' testimonies

two lawyers' offices

two actresses' roles

two days' pay

five years' experience*

Add *'s* if the word does not end in *s*.

two men's dreams

two children's toys

---

* Although some grammarians have held that inanimate objects logically can't possess anything, many common expressions like these are considered acceptable. Other common expressions are *the company's assets, a dollar's worth, the sun's rays.* Some writers prefer *five years of experience, the assets of the company,* and so forth.

Exception: Some organizations, buildings, or titles of magazines are written with the apostrophe and some without. Check with the source for the exact spelling.

> American Bankers Association
>
> Teachers College
>
> Nurses Residence Hall
>
> *but*
>
> Boys' Clubs of America
>
> Ladies' Home Journal
>
> Mother's Day

Rule 20. To make a plural proper name possessive, add an apostrophe.

> I'd like you to meet the Smiths' new neighbors.
>
> She said she is the Finches' niece.

Apostrophes Indicating Contractions

Rule 21. Use an apostrophe to show that letters or numbers have been deleted.

> You've come a long way.
>
> You'll be in the class of '04.

☜ **NOTE:** Using *its* for *it's* and vice versa is one of the most frequently made errors in writing. Proofread your work to make sure you've used the right *its/it's*.

The word *it's* is a contraction for *it is* or *it has.*

> I know it's easy to give up smoking because I've tried it so often. (Mark Twain)
>
> If you watch a game, it's fun. If you play at it, it's recreation. If you work at it, it's golf. (Bob Hope)

The word *its* (believe it or not) means possession—belonging to *it*.

The dog wagged *its* tail (the tail that belonged to it).

It's easy to understand why *its/it's* is the most commonly made error. Apostrophes usually mean possession, but with *it's/its* the one without the apostrophe means possession and the one with the apostrophe is a contraction.

To catch this error, when you proofread, read all the *it'ses/itses* as *it is,* and eliminate the apostrophe if you don't really mean to say *it is.*

Rule 22. Keep in mind that the following words are already possessive. Never add an apostrophe or *'s* to them.

mine, yours, his, hers, its, ours, theirs

The following words are simply errors; they do not exist.

mine's, yours', hers', ours', theirs'

Apostrophes Indicating Plurals

Rule 23. Use an apostrophe and *s* to form plurals of abbreviations with periods.

Most of the L.L.B.'s I know do not practice law.

Rule 24. To prevent confusion, some letters, abbreviations, or words are made plural by adding an *'s* rather than just *s.*

He got four A's (not *As*).

He spent his career dotting the i's (not *is*).

No, you can't go out wearing your p.j.'s (not *p.j.s*).

Delete all those unnecessary *that's* from your writing.

Answers to Chapter Challenge

1. We had planned to drive to the conference together; however, we later decided to travel separately. (Rule 1.)
2. We entered the room on tiptoe; the baby was sleeping. (Rule 2.)
3. The conferences will take place in Rabat, Morocco; Tokyo, Japan, and Siena, Italy.

   or

   The conferences will take place in Rabat, Morocco; Tokyo, Japan, and Siena, Italy. (Rule 3.)
4. Dear Mr. Clark: (Rule 4.)
5. He had three items on the agenda:

   1. Explaining the results of the tests
   2. Announcing the new procedures
   3. Getting his bosses' agreement to fund the project (Rule 2.)

6. Within a single hour, the puppy had wreaked the following devastation: chewed the electric cord, pulled the tablecloth off the table, and eaten my son's pet gerbil.
7. Always keep in mind: Haste makes waste.
8. He described himself as "just a country boy."
9. I thought I heard him say, "Are you trying to intimidate me?"
10. I tried to read "Getting onto the Information Superhighway" in *Business Week*, but I fell asleep at the wheel.
11. One witness's testimony was so weak that we anticipated an acquittal.
12. It's difficult to put the chart in its proper place when the file room is locked except for two hours each day.
13. Please bring *only* one friend to the party.

    or

    Please bring **only** one friend to the party.

or

Please bring <u>only</u> one friend to the party.

14. This music should be played *molto adagio,* or very slowly.

    or

    This music should be played "molto adagio," or very slowly.

15. This is not incorrect, but *Mr. Jones's secretary functions as a corporate guard dog* is more commonly used.

5   *Still More Punctuation Parentheses, Dashes, Hyphens, Ellipses, Brackets*

When attention is entirely concentrated on punctuation, there is some fear that the conduct of business may suffer, and a proposal get through without being properly obstructed on its demerits.

—FRANCIS M. CORNFORD

If you've ever wondered . . .

- Does the period go before or after the parenthesis?
- Is there a way to show my reader that I've left some words out of a quotation—or added some?
- Can dashes be used in business writing?

. . . you'll find the answers in this chapter.

Chapter Challenge

Only two of these sentences use parentheses, dashes, hyphens, and apostrophes correctly. Can you identify them? The answers are on page 89. The explanation for each item can be found on the page—or pages—indicated.

1. Please mail the envelope (the one on the right-hand corner of my desk.) (Rule 3, page 83.)
2. Product testing was stopped in June, just after the first customer complaints were received. (See Figure 1, p.2.) (Rule 4, page 83.)
3. After we spoke with Joan (the woman who is in charge of the account) we paid the invoice. (Rule 2, Exception A, page 82.)
4. Even though I got the printer to work (it had been making peculiar sounds all morning), I knew it was only a matter of time before it would break down completely. (Rule 2, Exception A, page 82.)
5. All the people involved, namely, the parents, the teachers, the children, and the police, wanted to talk to the press. (Rule 7, page 85.)
6. Bob is going on another two day crash diet. (Rule 8, page 86.)
7. Elaine was working on a highly-leveraged deal. (Rule 9, page 86.)
8. His memo stated, "With your help, we can make this project proffitable (sic) in the next few quarters." (Rule 18, page 89.)

Parentheses

Parentheses are used to set aside peripheral comments—information the author believes is of less importance than the main text. In business and academic writing, parentheses are also used to refer the reader to figures or illustrations that expand on or clarify the text.

Rule 1. Use parentheses sparingly. Don't use them for important ideas.

Correct: The parentheses set aside a peripheral comment.

It will take us six weeks (or even more) to issue the report.

Poor usage: Important information is put in parentheses.

We identified the time it took to process a claim (ten minutes) and notified the supervisor (Ms. Rubin).

Good usage: Important information is integrated into the sentence.

We notified Ms. Rubin, the supervisor, that it takes ten minutes to process a claim.

Here are two basic rules—and two exceptions—for punctuating material in parentheses.

Rule 2. If a whole sentence is enclosed in parentheses, the period goes inside the parenthesis.

We have not yet determined where the funds were deposited. (We are still waiting for the bank to send us a copy of the endorsed checks.) As soon as we have the information, we will call you.

Exception A: If the sentence or phrase within the parentheses interrupts the flow of the main sentence, do not put a period after the parenthetical sentence and do not use a capital letter.

Although we were able to finish the report (we were lucky to have Jim's assistance), we didn't have time to proofread it.

The comma after the closing parenthesis is correct. Had the parenthetical comment not been there, the comma would have been placed after *report*. The parentheses bump the comma out of its usual place.

Exception B: If the parenthetical sentence requires an exclamation point or a question mark, put that mark inside the parentheses and do not use a capital letter.

> The fact that we finished the report on time (we drove it to Federa̱ Express at 8:30 P.M.!) still amazes me.

> The fact that we finished the report on time (did you hear about our late-night ride to Federal Express?) still amazes me.

Rule 3. If the material inside the parentheses is not a sentence by itself, put the period outside the closing parenthesis.

> *Correct:*
> Make a left at the first light (the one after the gas station).

Rule 4. Refer to figures, charts, and so forth in either of the following two styles. Both are correct.

> Sales almost doubled in the last six months (see Figure 2, p. 10).

> Sales almost doubled in the last six months. (See Figure 2, p. 10.)

Rule 5. The first time an abbreviation is given that may not already be familiar to the reader, explain it in parentheses. From that point on in the text you may use the acronym alone.

> A Capital Appropriations Request (CAP) must be filled out for each expenditure over $5,000. The CAP must be signed by the director and forwarded to Budget Planning by the first of the month.

DANGER: Do not put a comma before a parenthetical expression. (The parentheses act as commas; therefore, no additional comma is needed.)

Incorrect:

The suggested submission date, (actually the deadline) was March 1.

Correct:

The suggested submission date (actually the deadline) was March 1.

Also correct:

The suggested submission date, actually the deadline, was March 1.

Dashes

Dashes signify a break, a sudden shift. Used carefully, they can make your writing clearer and more interesting. Overdone, they can become an irritant. On a typewriter, dashes are formed by typing two hyphens (- -) without spaces before, after, or between the hyphens. Word processors allow you to select a dash (—) from a list of typographical symbols.

Rule 6. Use dashes instead of commas if you want to put a bit of drama in your writing.

The only reason I wear glasses is for little things, like driving my car—or finding it. (Woody Allen)

This town only had two seasons—winter and "Road Under Repair." (George Gobel)

If you want to deemphasize a phrase, use parentheses. If you want to emphasize it, use dashes.

She forgot the directions (including the exit on the turnpike) again.

She forgot the directions—including the exit on the turnpike—again.

Rule 7. Use dashes to promote clarity. Dashes are useful in a sentence like the following, when there is a need for several commas within one sentence.

Acceptable:

All the company plants, especially those in Middletown, Richmond, and Morristown, need to be overhauled.

Clearer:

All the company plants—especially those in Middletown, Richmond, and Morristown—need to be overhauled.

See page 49 for a similar use of dashes.

✍ **NOTE:** You can set aside one word, a group of words, or even a whole sentence in dashes. If a second sentence follows the dash, do not begin it with a capital letter.

We will be moving to the fifth floor—we can't wait to enjoy all that space!

Hyphens

The hyphens discussed in this section allow you to hook up two words together. The use of hyphens to break up words that fall at the end of a line of text is explained in Chapter 10, "Word-Division Dilemmas."

Rule 8. Use a hyphen to hook up two or more words that describe a word that follows.

> She attended a two-day seminar.
>
> He is an infant-formula manufacturer.
>
> She has a well-organized desk.
>
> She likes state-of-the-art equipment.
>
> Send me a follow-up report.

Note: The hyphen is not needed when the descriptive words come *after* the item being described. For example:

> She attended a seminar that lasted two days.
>
> He manufactures infant formula.
>
> Her desk is well organized.
>
> She likes equipment that is state of the art.
>
> Send me a report that follows up on this issue.

DANGER: Failure to put in a hyphen can lead to silly
                        sentences!

He is an infant formula manufacturer means that he is a tiny, tiny person who somehow manages to manufacture formulas. *He is an infant-formula manufacturer,* on the other hand, means that he is a manufacturer of infant formula.

Rachel is a small business consultant means that she is under 5'2". But if you really mean that Rachel consults with small businesses (ones that employ fewer than 50 people) you should write: *Rachel is a small-business consultant.*

Rule 9: Do not use a hyphen with *-ly* words that describe a word that follows.

Incorrect:
> We invested in a highly-rated company.

Correct:
We invested in a highly rated company.

Rule 10. Many words that were once written as hyphenated words are now written without a hyphen. Here are some guidelines.

Co: The trend is to delete the hyphen.

cooperate, coordinate, copilot, coauthor

Ex: Use the hyphen.

ex-ball player, ex-chairperson

Re: The trend is to write these words as one.

reconstruct, reapply, even reengineer

The best advice is the old one: Consult a current dictionary. Look first under *re*. Some dictionaries provide a list of *re-* words written as one word. If none is provided, look under the word in question. If it does not have its own listing, use a hyphen.

Elect (as a suffix): Use a hyphen.

President-elect

Emeritus (as a suffix): The trend is to delete the hyphen.

professor emeritus

Rule 11. Use a hyphen to prevent confusion.

Send me two 8-inch pipes.
I need six ¾-inch tapes.

Ellipses

An ellipsis is three periods that indicate a break in thought or material the writer has purposely omitted.

Rule 12. Use an ellipsis to indicate uncertainty or an abrupt change in thought.

Was this a good strategy . . . or a terrible mistake?

A dash could also be used for this purpose.

Was this a good strategy—or a terrible mistake?

Rule 13. Use three dots to indicate that words have been omitted from the middle of a sentence.

The regulation states that "company officials . . . must cosign the loan agreement."

(The original regulation stated that "company officials, regardless of their state of residence, must cosign the loan agreement.")

Rule 14. Use four dots to indicate that words have been omitted at the end of a sentence. (The first dot is the period for the sentence.)

The manager wrote that "each employee must select a benefit plan. . . ."

(The original memo stated that "each employee must select a benefit plan regardless of the number of years the employee has been employed by the company.")

Rule 15. Use an ellipsis to indicate a pause.

The guy who invented the first wheel was an idiot. The guy who invented the other three . . . he was a genius. (Sid Caesar)

A dash could also be used.

Brackets

Rule 16. Use brackets as parentheses within a parenthetical element.

The court has found that the carrier has no liability in this case. (See Federal Register 407B [referred to in Johnson's letter of January 6] for a full explanation.)

Rule 17. Use brackets to indicate when you want to add something, usually a word or phrase of explanation, to make the author's meaning clearer.

Marlene stated that "she [Tom's partner] had played the critical role in making the sale."

Rule 18. Use brackets to enclose the Latin word *sic*, meaning, essentially, "The mistake you see here is not mine; that's the way it was in the original."

The letter of recommendation stated, "John is an inteligent [*sic*] person who has become an important part of our team."

Answers to Chapter Challenge

1. Incorrect. Please mail the envelope (the one on the right-hand corner of my desk).
2. Correct. *Also correct:* Product testing was stopped in June, just after the first customer complaints were received (see Figure 1, p.2).
3. Incorrect. After we spoke with Joan (the woman who is in charge of the account), we paid the invoice.
4. Correct.
5. Incorrect. All the people involved—namely, the parents, the teachers, the children, and the police—wanted to talk to the press.
6. Incorrect. Bob is going on another two-day crash diet.
7. Incorrect. Elaine was working on a highly leveraged deal.
8. His memo stated, "With your help, we can make this project proffitable [*sic*] in the next few quarters."

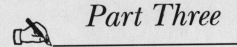

Part Three

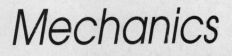

Mechanics

6 Twelve Rules for Handling Numbers

When angry, count four; when very angry, swear.

—MARK TWAIN

Let's see. You write out numbers from one to ten and use figures for numbers over ten. But what if numbers above and below ten appear in the same sentence? And should I write $4.3 million or $4,300,000.00? If questions like this come up as you write—read on.

Chapter Challenge

Read each item below and decide whether the numbers are handled correctly in each sentence. To find an explanation of each item, see the page number listed after each item. The answers are on page 97.

1. I posed three questions to the four accountants and 12 financial planners. (Rule 4, page 94.)
2. The profits had increased from $2.3 million to $4,000,000.00 in just five years. (Rule 5, page 95.)
3. One hundred out of 122 lawyers who read the brief sided with the defendant. (Rule 6, page 95.)

4. I would like to order six, one-inch nails. (Rule 7 and Rule 9, page 96.)
5. His new address is 402 E. 8th St. (Rule 12, page 97.)
6. Please renew my subscription for three (3) years. (Rule 11, page 96.)

Rule 1. In general writing and formal business writing, use words for numbers 1 through 10; use figures for numbers over 10.

I look forward to meeting your ten staff assistants. They will file the 11 committee reports.

Rule 2. In technical writing and informal business writing, figures are often used for all numbers because they stand out more emphatically.

We are enclosing 3 samples to be tested.

Rule 3. In high school and college papers and in newspapers and magazines, spell out numbers that can be expressed in one or two words. Use figures for numbers that cannot be expressed in one or two words. (Hyphenated words are considered one word.)

Isaac Asimov, one of the most prolific authors of all time, wrote thirty-eight science fiction novels and published over 470 works altogether.

Rule 4. When numbers above and below 10 are used in one sentence, express related items in a consistent manner.

At the meeting, 5 accountants, 12 auditors, and 3 financial analysts voted against the plan. (Numbers of professionals in the various groups are related.)

At the meeting, 5 accountants, 12 auditors, and 3 financial analysts pointed out three errors in the budget. (The number of errors is not related to the number of professionals.)

Rule 5. Write related numbers in a similar fashion. Use the preferred method for millions; it's clearer.

Incorrect:
Gross revenue in the first quarter was $4,300,000 and $3 million in the second.

Correct:
Gross revenue in the first quarter was $4,300,000 and $3,000,000 in the second.

Preferred:
Gross revenue in the first quarter was $4.3 million and $3.0 million in the second.

Rule 6. Never begin a sentence with a figure.

Incorrect:
23 separate issues were discussed.

Correct:
Twenty-three separate issues were discussed.

Exception: When preparing slides or transparencies, you may use this style:

The first quarter results showed:

- 4% decrease in manufacturing costs
- 2% increase in gross profits

When a sentence begins with a number, and a related number appears in the sentence, use one of these styles:

Correct:
Forty-eight out of 52 officers described the meeting as a valuable use of their time.

Also correct and clearer:
Of the 52 officers, 48 described the meeting as a valuable use of their time.

Rule 7. When two numbers fall next to each other in a sentence, write out one and use a figure for the other.

I need four 3-ring binders.

John will buy twelve 6-foot boards.

Note there is no comma between *four* and *3-ring*. (Rule 28, page 52, explains why.)

Rule 8. Use figures for parts of a book.

Chapter 3

page 4

figure 8A

Rule 9. Use figures for time, measurement, or money. For the exception, see the next rule.

4 o'clock or 4:00 (NOT four o'clock)

4 × 6 feet

7 yards

Rule 10. In formal writing, such as invitations or proclamations, spell out all numbers.

the twenty-sixth of August, nineteen hundred and ninety-five

Rule 11. In legal documents, such as contracts, numbers are written in both figures and words.

The fee for each consultation is one hundred and seventy-five dollars ($175).

It is unnecessary—and a bit silly—to use the legal style in business writing.

General writing and formal business writing:
Please have three telephone lines installed in room 4072.

Technical writing and informal business writing:
Please have 3 telephone lines installed in room 4072.

Unnecessary and silly:

Please have three (3) telephone lines installed in room 4072.

Rule 12. Follow Rule 1 for numbers in street names—use words for numbers 1-10, use figures for numbers above 10.

1422 Second Ave. (NOT 1422 2nd Ave.)

605 East 210th St.

The words *avenue* and *street* are commonly abbreviated on the inside address of a letter, though these words are spelled out in formal situations, such as a wedding invitation.

Answers to Chapter Challenge

1. Incorrect. I posed three questions to the 4 accountants and 12 financial planners.
2. Incorrect. The profits had increased from $2.3 million to $4.0 million in just five years.
3. Correct—but see a better way on page 95 under Rule 6.
4. Incorrect. I would like to order six 1-inch nails.
5. Incorrect. His new address is 402 E. Eighth St.

   or

   402 E. Eighth Street.
6. Incorrect. Please renew my subscription for three years.

7 Spelling Bee

> He respects Owl, because you can't help
> respecting anybody who can spell TUESDAY,
> even if he doesn't spell it right; but spelling
> isn't everything. There are days when
> spelling Tuesday simply doesn't count.
>
> —A. A. MILNE, *The World of Pooh*

I begin this chapter of the book with a sigh. Every rule of spelling has so many exceptions that one wonders whether any of our spelling rules deserve the name *rule*.

Consider this most-remembered rule of spelling:

> *I* before *E* except after *C*
> Or when sounded like *A*
> As in *neighbor* and *weigh*

OK, but what about *height? seize? counterfeit? weird?* There you have it. Our "best" is bogus.

Therefore, I've limited this chapter to rules that have relatively few exceptions. Following the Chapter Challenge, you'll find useful rules to help you change verb forms and make plurals. I think you'll find Rules 4 and 5 particularly helpful.

Chapter Challenge

Circle the correct spelling. The answers are on page 106. The spelling rule for each item can be found on the page indicated.

1. The plural of *memo* is (memos, memoes). (Rule 4, page 102.)
2. The plural of *synthesis* is (synthesises, syntheses). (Rule 6, page 103.)
3. The plural of *memorandum* is (memoranda, memorandas). (Rule 6, Other Borrowed Words, page 103.)
4. The plural of *leave of absence is* (leaves of absence, leave of absences). (Rule 5, page 103.)
5. The past tense of *refer* is (refered, referred). (Rule 1, page 101.)
6. The past tense of *travel* is (traveled, travelled). (Rule 1, page 101.)
7. The plural of the family name *Smith* is (Smiths, Smith's). (Rule 9, page 104.)
8. The Supreme Court's decision of October 1 (superceeds, supercedes, supersedes) all other decisions. (Note, Rule 1, page 101.)
9. Which is the correct spelling of what Sears Roebuck used to produce? (catalog, catalogue) (New Spellings, page 105.)

Suggestions for Better Spelling

Before I list the rules I have found helpful, I have a few suggestions for those who wish to become better spellers.

1. Keep a list of the words you know you don't know and then make up a mnemonic to help you remember the most frequently used words. (I've always remembered that *occa-*

sion has one *s* because a teacher once said that if we put two *s's* in it, we'd make *asses* of ourselves. This was such a risqué remark coming out of my very straight-laced ninth-grade English teacher that I never forgot it.)

2. Buy a bad speller's dictionary. It lists the word the way bad spellers might spell it and then gives you the correct spelling.

3. Use the spell check feature on your word processor. Even if you think you're a good speller, it will highlight errors. Of course, the spell check won't pick up certain kinds of errors—it doesn't know you meant to write *I enjoyed reading your letter* when in fact you wrote *I enjoyed reading you letter.* The latter looks just fine to your spell check.

4. Befriend a colleague at work who is a good speller and get him or her to proofread your most important memos and letters.

A Special Note for Bad Spellers

There is no direct relationship between the ability to spell and intelligence. Good spellers have good visual memory; it's a gift. (The good spellers can also probably remember who sat in front of, behind, and across from them in third grade.) Don't let the good spellers intimidate you! Remember, no one has ever written on a college or job application: "Excellent speller—frequent winner of spelling bees in grades 1–6, Pleasantville Elementary School."

Just to Refresh Your Memory

Most words form the plural by adding an *s* (like *rose, roses*); words ending in *s, x, ch, sh* form the plural by adding *es* (like *bus, buses*). Some words do their own thing (like *child, children*).

Here are 15 rules that have relatively few exceptions.

To Double or Not to Double

Is it *committed* or *commited, refered* or *referred, traveled* or *travelled?**

Rule 1. Double the final consonant when adding an ending that begins with a vowel (*ed, er, ing*) if all three of the following are true:

1. The word ends in a single consonant.
2. The consonant is preceded by a single vowel (*a, e, i, o,* or *u*).
3. The accent is on the last syllable *or* the word has only one syllable.

Consider *commit.* Is it *commited* or *committed?*

1. The last letter is a single consonant (*t*).
2. The consonant is preceded by a single vowel (*i*).
3. The accent is on the last syllable.

The correct spelling is *committed.*

Using this system with *refer* produces the same result. But *travel* does not meet our third criterion. The accent is on the first syllable (TRA-vel). Therefore, the correct word is *traveled.*

◻ NOTE: With words that end in the sound *seed,* keep these facts in mind:

Only 1 word ends in *sede: supersede.*
Only 3 words end in *ceed: exceed, proceed, succeed.*
Everything else is *cede: precede, secede, recede, intercede, accede.*

---

* British spelling does not follow these rules. For more on British spellings, see page 106.

Two Rules for Y

Rule 2. If a consonant comes before the *y,* change *y* to *ies.*

copy	copies
story	stories
injury	injuries

Rule 3. If a vowel comes before the *y,* just add *s.*

attorney	attorneys
valley	valleys

Two Rules for O and a Couple of Exceptions

Rule 4. If a vowel comes before the *o,* add *s.*

ratio	ratios
folio	folios
studio	studios

If a consonant comes before the *o,* sometimes you add an *s* and sometimes an *es.* Unfortunately, only memorizing the correct spelling works with these.

memo	memos
solo	solos
zero	zeros (also zeroes)
but	
potato	potatoes
hero	heroes
cargo	cargoes (also cargos)

This explains the Dan Quayle spelling-bee disaster. A fourth grader was asked to spell *potato.* He spelled it correctly, *p-o-t-a-t-o.* However, the then Vice President prevailed upon the young man to add an *e,* thus forming *potatoe.* Apparently, Mr. Quayle remembered that the *plural* of that vegetable was *potatoes* and assumed that the singular ended in *e.* It doesn't.

Rule 5. Most hyphenated words or closely associated words are made plural by making the main noun plural.

father-in-law	fathers-in-law (NOT father-in-laws)
leave of absence	leaves of absence
runner-up	runners-up (NOT runner-ups)
deputy chief of staff	deputy chiefs of staff

Beware, however. Some compound nouns don't follow that rule.

six-year-olds

drive-ins

When in doubt, consult your dictionary.

Rule 6. Nouns that come from Latin or Greek and end in *is* form the plural by changing the *i* to *e*.

axis	axes
diagnosis	diagnoses
basis	bases
analysis	analyses
synthesis	syntheses
crisis	crises
parenthesis	parentheses

Other Borrowed Words

Here are other singular and plural forms of words derived from other languages. Where there is more than one accepted spelling, the preferred one is listed first. Note that in some cases an English usage has gained acceptance along with, or in preference to, the plural form of the original language.

memorandum	memoranda *or* memorandums (NOT memorandas)
medium	media *or* mediums
colloquium	colloquia

nucleus	nuclei
vertebra	vertebrae
alumnus (masculine)	alumni
alumna (feminine)	alumnae
monsieur	messieurs
bureau	bureaus
formula	formulae *or* formulas
index	indices *or* indexes
concerto	concerti *or* concertos

Rule 7. Note the plurals for these common expressions:

dos and don'ts

yeses and noes

pros and cons

ins and outs

ups and downs

Rule 8. Make the year and other numbers plural by adding an *s.*

the 1990s

a salary in the low 40s

An apostrophe and *s* can also be used.

Rule 9. Make family names that do not end in *s* plural by adding an *s,* not an apostrophe and *s.*

Incorrect:
The Smith's will be here later.

Correct:
The Smiths will be here later.

Rule 10. If a family name ends in *s, x, ch, sh,* or *z,* add *es* to make it plural. If a family name ends in a vowel (*a, e, i, o,* or u), add *s,* not *es.*

| Mr. and Mrs. Jones | The Joneses |

Remember the phrase *keeping up with the Joneses.* (NOT the Jones!)

Mr. and Mrs. Cass	The Casses
Mr. and Mrs. Fox	The Foxes
Mr. and Mrs. French	The Frenches
Mr. and Mrs. Marsh	The Marshes
Mr. and Mrs. Pirelli	The Pirellis

Do not add *es* if doing so makes the name difficult to pronounce.

| Mr. and Mrs. Hodges | The Hodges (NOT the Hodgeses) |
| Mr. and Mrs. Estes | The Estes (NOT the Esteses) |

New Spellings

A variety of new spellings are making their way into our dictionaries. My *Random House Unabridged* lists *lite* as "an informal simplified spelling of *light.*" *Nite* and *thru* have similar entries.

Of course, we don't spell the words this new way in business writing, but in a personal letter or a note you might.

Some words can be spelled two ways with impunity. The word *dialogue*, for example, can also be spelled *dialog*. How do I know this? Recently, I saw the word *dialogue* spelled as *dialog* in an article. "Oops! Typo!" I said. Then I saw the same "misspelling" someplace else. I looked it up in the dictionary, but there was no entry under *dialog*. Then I looked at *dialogue*. After the definitions were these two words: "Also, *dialog*." That means that *dialog* is an acceptable alternate spelling. Most people do not spell it that way, but enough do to have earned it a place in the dictionary. Other words that are losing the *gue* are *monologue* (*monolog*) and *catalogue* (*catalog*). And *cigaret* is now an acceptable spelling of *cigarette*.

British Versus American Spelling

Over the past two hundred years English and American spelling have diverged in very specific ways. Here are some of the differences.

	American	**British**
-or, -our	honor	honour
	color	colour
-er, -re	theater	theatre
	center	centre
l, ll	traveled	travelled
	counseled	counselled
s, z	exercise	exercize
z, s	organization	organisation
	legalization	legalisation

For those of you who have difficulty spelling, remember this quote of President Andrew Jackson: "It's a damn poor mind that can think of only one way to spell a word."

Answers to Chapter Challenge

1. memos
2. syntheses
3. memoranda
4. leaves of absence
5. referred
6. traveled
7. Smiths
8. supersedes
9. Each is correct.

8 Capitalization Questions

"Well," said Owl, "the customary procedure
in such cases is as follows."

"What does Crustimoney Proseedcake
mean?" said Pooh. "For I am a Bear of Very
Little Brain, and long words Bother me."

"It means the Thing to Do."

—A. A. MILNE, *Winnie-the-Pooh*

Capital letters attract attention. That's why we use them for names of people, places, and things. But what about job titles, titles of reports, names of business forms? Are these capitalized?

Take this Chapter Challenge to determine if you are using capital letters in accordance with today's standards for capitalization.

Chapter Challenge

Capital letters are used correctly in 5 out of 13 items. Can you find them? See the rule referred to for an explanation of each item. The answers are on page 113.

1. We would like to recognize Barbara Sanchez for her outstanding Attendance Record. (Rule 1, Danger, page 109.)

2. We were surprised that Vice President Lifton refused to answer the question. (Rule 2, page 109.)

3. The Senior Vice President, Dan Porter, made a site visit last week. (Rule 2, page 109.)

4. For more than ten years, she worked in Accounts Payable. (Rule 5, page 110.)

5. We lived in the East for three years and then moved to the South. (Rule 8, page 111.)

6. Last Summer we took a trip with the whole family; what a mistake! (Rule 9, page 111.)

7. She wrote an article for the *Journal of Mediocrity* entitled "Smith is Runner-up Again." (Rule 10, page 111.)

8. Mechanical inventions proliferated in the late Nineteenth Century. (Rule 13, page 112.)

9. In college I took a course in Playwriting. (Rule 14, page 112.)

10. This was his guiding principle: get them before they get you. (Rule 15, page 112.)

11. Caution: Angry boss on the other side of this door. (Rule 16, page 113.)

12. Please return the Dividend Reinvestment form in the envelope provided. (Rule 17, page 113.)

13. The surge in profits can be seen in Figure 5 on page 2. (Rule 18, page 113.)

The problem in capitalization is more often sins of commission than sins of omission. People tend to add capital letters where they are not needed, rather than fail to place them where they are needed. Read Rule 1 and the Danger note carefully.

Rule 1. Do not capitalize words only because you wish to lend them importance. Remember, only names of specific people, cities, and companies are capitalized. (Many corporations do not follow this rule or the following one. Check with your executive officer to determine your company's style for capitalization.)

Chemical Bank takes pride in announcing the opening of a new branch. The *bank* now has more than 40 branches in Brooklyn. (NOT The *Bank* now has . . .)

Texaco is committed to providing its customers with the best service possible. Therefore, the *company* trains each person who has customer contact very carefully. (NOT Therefore, the *Company* trains each . . .)

Exception: The word *bank* or *company* should be capitalized only in legal documents, formal contracts, and policy statements.

Chemical Bank (referred to hereafter as "the Bank") provides employees with a flexible benefits program. On September 1 of each year, the Bank distributes a Benefits Election Form to all employees.

DANGER: Ads often contain words that are capitalized only to attract the reader's eye. Do not follow this practice except when writing advertising copy.

Acceptable in ads:
First National Bank—known for Quality and Service.

Incorrect in general writing:
We will be conducting a Performance Appraisal next week. Our emphasis this year is on Quality.

Correct:
We will be conducting a performance appraisal next week. Our emphasis this year is on quality.

Rule 2. Capitalize job titles when the title precedes a person's name and when no comma separates the title from the person's name.

Vice President Caputo addressed the trainees last Monday.

but

The vice president, Michael Caputo, addressed the trainees last Monday.

Rule 3. Do not capitalize job titles when they stand alone or are placed after the person's name.

Michael Caputo, vice president, addressed the trainees.

I saw the personnel director in the hall. She's a senior vice president with the company.

DANGER: Many companies do not follow these rules; they capitalize all job titles whenever they appear. Follow your company's preference in this matter.

Rule 4. The only job titles that always require capitalization are those of officials of international bodies, countries, and states. Local officials' titles are usually not capitalized, unless they precede the person's name.

The President arrived yesterday at 10:00 A.M. (The person referred to could be the President of the United States, the President of Mexico, and so forth.)

The mayor arrived yesterday at 10:00 A.M. (*But:* Mayor Hodges was two hours late.)

Rule 5. Capitalize names of departments, unless your company does not do so.

She used to work in Human Resources.

She used to work in human resources.

Rule 6. Capitalize the first word of each item in a list.

Please be prepared to discuss:

- The steps your unit has taken to increase quality
- The costs of these steps
- Any obstacles you had to overcome to implement the changes

Rule 7. Capitalize *the* if it is the first word of the title of a book, film, poem, or other literary work, or a legal document. However, in periodicals and in some organizations, *the* can remain lowercase even though it is part of the formal title.

> I loved reading Shakespeare's *The Tempest.*

> To keep up on current events, I read *The New York Times* [*or:* the *New York Times*] and the *National Inquirer.*

Rule 8. Capitalize *north, east, south,* and *west* only when they refer to a part of the country, not a general direction.

> She loves living in the West.

> *but*

> Go west one block.

Rule 9. Do not capitalize the names of seasons.

> I will see you in the fall.

Rule 10. In titles, capitalize important words (including verbs and hyphenated words) or words with five or more letters.

> The report was entitled High-Impact Aerobics for Octogenarians.

> The seminar title was Up-to-Date Inventory Management. (*To* is not an important word.)

Rule 11. In a series of questions, capitalization is optional.

> Are we to move ahead quickly? Proceed at a normal pace? Drag our feet?

> *or*

> Are we to move ahead quickly? proceed at a normal pace? drag our feet?

Rule 12. Brand names are capitalized, although they tend to lose their capital letters as they become part of our everyday speech.

I have a Xerox copier.

Can you get a xerox of that article?

Companies don't want to see their brand names lose their capitals. That's why you will often see the mark ® next to a word. That identifies the name as a trademark that can only be used as it appears in the ad—with the capital letters.

Rule 13. Names of countries and historic periods are capitalized, centuries are not.

He is the ambassador to France.

Dickens wrote about the effects of the Industrial Revolution.

The twenty-first century (NOT Twenty-First Century) presents new challenges.

Rule 14. Names of courses of study are not capitalized unless they refer to a specific course or to a language.

I am requesting tuition reimbursement for a course in microbiology.

I am requesting tuition reimbursement for Microbiology 101.

I am taking a course in Spanish this semester. The exact course title is Spanish 101.

Rule 15. When one sentence serves to introduce a second sentence, the sentences are joined by a colon. If the second sentence is the main point, begin it with a capital letter.

She kept emphasizing this point: No matter what arguments were presented, the division would most likely move to Atlanta.

Our overtime was due to one factor: We had not properly taught the machinists how to repair the equipment.

If the words that follow the colon do not constitute a sentence, do not use a capital letter.

> She had only one thing on her mind: getting to the baseball game on time.

Rule 16. Use a capital letter after the words *Note* or *Caution*.

> Note: Unless you have your invitation with you, you will not be admitted.

Rule 17. In business correspondence, capitalize the full name of an official form plus the word *form*.

Incorrect:

> I am enclosing a Change of Beneficiary form (form IL-7) for you to complete.

> I am enclosing a change of beneficiary form (form IL-7) for you to complete.

Correct:

> I am enclosing a Change of Beneficiary Form (Form IL-7) for you to complete.

Rule 18. Generally, but not always, the words *figure, table, and illustration* are capitalized; the word *page* is not.

> The new office layout is pictured in Figure 3A on page 7.

> *or*

> The new office layout is pictured in figure 3A on page 7.

Answers to Chapter Challenge

1. Incorrect
2. Correct
3. Incorrect

4. Correct—*accounts payable* is also correct.

5. Correct

6. Incorrect

7. Incorrect—"Smith Is Runner-Up Again"

8. Incorrect

9. Incorrect

10. Incorrect

11. Correct

12. Incorrect

13. Correct—figure 5 is also correct.

9 Brief Words on Abbreviations

> Dear School: Please eckuse John being absent on Jan. 28, 29, 30, 31, 32, and also 33.
>
> —STUDENT'S ABSENCE NOTE, QUOTED BY
> RICHARD LEDERER IN *Anguished English*

Abbreviations are everywhere: the IRS, IBM, the FDA, Ph.D.'s, M.D.'s, I.O.U.'s, and so forth. Some of the abbreviations have periods; some had them and lost them. In fact, the trend today is toward dropping the periods.

Chapter Challenge

True or False? The answers are on page 118. The rule that governs each issue is listed after each item.

1. It is considered acceptable to abbreviate the months of the year except in business and academic writing. (Rule 3, page 116.)
2. The plural of the abbreviation *CEO* is *CEOs*. (Rule 5, page 116.)
3. The plural of the abbreviation *Ms.* is *Mss.* (Rule 7, page 117.)

4. The plural of the abbreviation for *pages* is *pp.* (Rule 9, page 117.)

5. This sentence is punctuated correctly: I will meet you at 4:00 P.M.. (Note, page 117.)

   Extra Credit:

6. What is the plural of the abbreviation for *Miss*? (Rule 7, page 117.)

Rule 1. Use the U.S. Postal Service's two-letter state abbreviations on the envelope. No period should follow the abbreviation. It is preferable to spell out the state name or use the uppercase and lowercase abbreviations in the inside address of the letter.

Missouri	MO	Mo.
Kansas	KS	Kans.
Pennsylvania	PA	Pa.

Rule 2. In the inside address of a letter, you may abbreviate *avenue* and *street*. This is done routinely today in all but the most formal situations, such as wedding announcements.

Rule 3. Avoid abbreviating months. Do so only in tables or when space is limited.

Rule 4. Make abbreviations with periods plural by adding an apostrophe and *s*.

Five Ph.D.'s are attending the conference.

Two of the packages we received were c.o.d.'s.

Rule 5. Make abbreviations without periods plural by adding only an *s*.

The four CEOs are CPAs.

Rule 6. Use an apostrophe and *s* if providing an *s* alone would be confusing.

Be sure to dot all the *i*'s and cross all the *t*'s (not *is* and *ts*).

Rule 7. Follow the chart below for plural forms of titles.

Singular	*Plural*
Mr.	Messrs.
Ms.	Mses. *or* Mss.
Mrs.	Mmes.

(*Miss* is not an abbreviation. The plural is *Misses*. This form is rarely used today.)

Rule 8. Make most abbreviations plural by adding *s*.

bldg.	bldgs.
vol.	vols.
co.	cos.
No.	Nos.
Dr.	Drs.

Rule 9. Make some single-letter abbreviations plural by doubling the letter.

p. 18 (page 18)	pp. 18–23 (pages 18 through 23)
l. 20 (line 20)	ll. 40–45 (lines 40 through 45)

NOTE: If a sentence ends in an abbreviation, the period after the abbreviation serves also as the period for the sentence.

Incorrect:

I will see you in the lobby at 2:30 P.M..

Correct:

I will see you in the lobby at 2:30 P.M.

Answers to Chapter Challenge

1. False. As a rule, do not abbreviate months except in tables or when space is limited.

2. True

3. True—*Mses.* is also acceptable.

4. True

5. False

Extra Credit:

6. There is no abbreviation for *Miss;* hence there is no plural of it!

10 Word-Division Dilemmas

Alice B. Toklas and Gertrude Stein were
both American ex-patriots.

—STUDENT PAPER, QUOTED BY RICHARD
LEDERER IN *Anguished English*

The best advice on dividing a word at the end of a line is, don't.
First, hyphenated words are difficult to read; they slow the
reader down. Second, studies show that people are more at-
tracted to, and thus more likely to read, material presented with
what is called a *ragged* or unjustified right margin. That is probably because a ragged margin looks homemade compared to the
straight margin used in books, magazines, and newsletters. However, if you must hyphenate because your text must be justified
(that is, the margin on the right must be as straight as the one on
the left), follow the guidelines in this chapter.

First, tackle the Chapter Challenge on hyphens.

Chapter Challenge

Which is the preferred hyphenation for each item? See page 121
for the answers. The rule number cited explains each usage
issue.

1. region-al	*or*	re-gional	(Rule 2, page 120.)
2. cam-era	*or*	camer-a	(Rule 1, page 120.)
3. tell-ing	*or*	tel-ling	(Rule 2, Exception, page 120.)
4. Josh-ua	*or*	Joshu-a	(Rule 1, page 120.)
5. speak-er	*or*	spea-ker	(Rule 1, page 120.)

Rule 1. Do not hyphenate:

- Words of fewer than six letters
- Words of only one syllable
- A word so that the letters *-er* or *-ed* are on the second line (Do not write *tell-er, walk-ed.*)
- A word so that one syllable is left on a line (Do not write *a-pologize, criteri-a.*)
- An abbreviation
- A contraction
- A person's name
- The last word on a page
- Two lines in a row
- Many lines on one page
- Words that are already hyphenated like *self-interest* or *ex-mayor*

Rule 2. If you must hyphenate:

- Divide the word as far into the word as possible. It's easier to read *congratu-late* than *con-gratulate.* That's because the reader can guess and complete the word before looking at the next line.
- Divide words between double consonants, again as far into the word as possible. *Recom-mend* is better than *rec-ommend.* (*Exception:* If a word consists of a root word and a prefix or suffix, divide the word so that the root word stands alone: thus *call-ing,* not *cal-ling.*)
- Consult a dictionary. Identifying where syllables begin and end is difficult.

☜ **NOTE:** If you must use justified print, determine whether your word processor automatically hyphenates words. If it does, check your copy. Make sure that no two consecutive lines end in hyphens. You can cancel the feature if you find that it causes more problems than it solves.

Answers to Chapter Challenge

1. region-al
2. cam-era
3. tell-ing
4. Neither is acceptable.
5. Do not hyphenate.

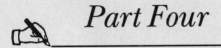

Part Four

Grammar

11 *Pronoun Problems*

> Guilt, vengeance, and bitterness can be emotionally destructive to you and your children. You must get rid of them.
>
> —RICHARD LEDERER, *Anguished English,*
>
> GIVING AN EXAMPLE OF PRONOUN MISUSE

Pronouns cause problems almost as soon as we begin to speak. Most children's first sentence sounds something like this: "Me want that" (usually pronounced *dat*). However, by age two or so, all native speakers of English of normal intelligence say, "I want that." We all learn that *me* is the wrong word. We are not taught this; we hear it and assimilate it. We learn that although three pronouns stand for our individuality (*me, myself,* and *I*), only *I* can be used as subject of a sentence.

But pronoun problems still crop up—especially when a sentence contains more than one proper name or pronoun.

Chapter Challenge

Which items are correct? The answers are on page 133. To find an explanation of each pronoun issue, see the page listed after each item.

1. Jim and myself have studied the manual carefully. (Rule 1, pages 126–131.)

2. Please expect a call from either Lorinda or myself next week. (Rule 1, pages 126–131.)
3. Thank you for explaining the new system to Robert and I. (Rule 1, pages 126–131.)
4. It's a private matter between Kate and I. (Rule 2, page 131.)
5. Me and him are buddies. (Rule 1, pages 126–131.)
6. They are more knowledgeable in that area than us. (Rule 3, page 132.)
7. Our director was not sure that Fred and myself could attend the meeting. (Rule 1, pages 126–131.)
8. She was told by the doorman that Sally and her had left an hour before. (Rule 1, pages 126–131.)
9. Please give Bob or I the key to the desk drawer. (Rule 1, pages 126–131.)
10. I knew that Frank and myself had made a computation error. (Rule 1, pages 126–131.)

Here are tips and tricks that will enable you to select the correct pronoun. Since pronouns cause so many problems, we added quizzes within this chapter so you can check your pronoun proficiency.

Rule 1. Remove other people's names and the word *and* from the sentence to determine the correct pronoun. Then reform the sentence; the correct pronoun choice will be obvious. In the examples below, the correct usage is checked.

Pronouns as Subjects

Problem:
Rita, John, and (I, me, myself) attended the conference.

Possibilities:
Me attended the conference.

Myself attended the conference.

✓ *I attended the conference.*

Correct:
Rita, John, and I attended the conference.

Problem:
   In the morning Charlie and (he, him) will go to Boston.

Possibilities:
✓ In the morning *he* will go to Boston.

   In the morning *him* will go to Boston.

Correct:
   In the morning Charlie and he will go to Boston.

Problem:
   Alex and (they, them) deserve a chance.

Possibilities:
✓ *They* deserve a chance.

   Them deserve a chance.

Correct:
   Alex and they deserve a chance.

Problem:
   (She, Her) and Sarah are friends of mine.

Change *are* to *is* first, since we will be trying out the sentence
with a singular subject rather than a plural one.

Possibilities:
   Her is a friend of mine.

✓ *She* is a friend of mine.

Correct:
   She and Sarah are friends of mine.

Problem:
   Mr. Street, Ms. Franz, and (he, him) were committed to
   the project.

Change *were* to *was* first.

Possibilities:
✓ *He* was committed to the project.

   Him was committed to the project.

Correct:

Mr. Street, Ms. Franz, and he were committed to the project.

Exercise

Circle the correct pronouns.

1. (She, Her) and (I, me) reviewed the proposal and agreed on the format.
2. The West Coast branch and (we, us) have a different point of view on the contract.
3. The report said that John and (he, him) were the star performers.
4. The executive committee and (she, her) have picked a new department manager.
5. The outside consultants and (they, them) will make the presentation at noon.

Answers: 1. She, I; 2. we; 3. he; 4. she; 5. they.

Other Pronoun Uses

Problem:

She gave Bob and (I, me, myself) the directions to the Chicago office.

Possibilities:

She gave *I* the directions to the Chicago office.

✓ She gave *me* the directions to the Chicago office.

She gave *myself* the directions to the Chicago office.

Correct:

She gave Bob and me the directions to the Chicago office.

A Special Note About Myself

You have probably noticed that *myself* has not been the correct answer in any of the examples so far. Here's why.

There are only two reasons to use the word *myself:* for emphasis and to show that you did something to yourself. Note that *myself* is used along with *I* in each sentence.

> *I* collected all the data *myself.*
>
> When Allen came to manage our unit, everyone said he was wonderful. *I myself* wasn't sure. (No commas are needed.)
>
> *I'm* going to sit right down and write *myself* a letter.
>
> *I* could have killed *myself* when I learned how much money I had lost.

Problem:
> We appreciate the high quality of the work you've done for Frank and (he, him).

Possibilities:
> We appreciate the high quality of the work you've done for *he.*
>
> ✓ We appreciate the high quality of the work you've done for *him.*

Correct:
> We appreciate the high quality of the work you've done for Frank and him.

Exercise

Circle the correct pronouns.

1. The report was written by Tom and (I, me).
2. She looked at Harry and (I, me) and smiled.
3. Please do not ask Linda or (she, her) any more questions.
4. Give Frank and (I, me) a break!
5. Please address your questions to Max and (myself, me).

Answers: 1. me; 2. me; 3. her; 4. me; 5. me.

Use the same system in long, complicated sentences.

Problem:

I was told by a confidential source that the manufacturer and (he, him) had colluded on the price.

Possibilities:

✓ I was told by a confidential source that *he* had colluded on the price.

I was told by a confidential source that *him* had colluded on the price.

Answer:

I was told by a confidential source that the manufacturer and he had colluded on the price.

Problem:

The chairperson was unsure whether Bob Clark, Jean Nelson, and (she, her) had given the client and (they, them) the estimate.

Possibilities:

The chairperson was unsure whether *her* had given ...

✓ The chairperson was unsure whether *she* had given ...

... she had given *they* ....

✓ ... she had given *them* ....

Answer:

The chairperson was unsure whether Bob Clark, Jean Nelson, and she had given the client and them the estimate.

Problem:

(We, Us) employees should not assume that (he, him) and (they, them) have been completely forthright.

Possibilities:

Us should not assume ...

✓ *We* should not assume ...

✓ . . . he has been completely forthright.

. . . *him* has been completely forthright.

✓ . . . *they* have been completely forthright.

. . . *them* have been completely forthright.

Answer:
We employees should not assume that he and they have been completely forthright.

Between you and I, him, her, us, *and* them

Rule 2. Use the following words with *between: me, him, her, us*, and *them*. There are no exceptions.

Incorrect:
Between you and I

Between we and they

Between she and I

Correct:
Between you and me

Between us and them

Between her and me

Exercise

Circle the correct pronouns.

1. You must never try to get between (they, them) and (we, us).
2. Between you and (I, me), I see no reason not to go home early today.
3. The difference between Jack and (I, me) is the difference between mediocrity and excellence.

4. The terms of the contract were kept between the lawyer and (they, them).

5. Don't even get between (he, him) and his brother.

Answers: 1. them, us; 2. me; 3. me; 4. them; 5. him.

Rule 3. After the words *than* or *as* in comparisons, determine the correct pronoun by mentally adding any missing words to the sentence.

Problem:
She is taller than (I, me).

With added words:
She is taller than I am.

Correct:
She is taller than I.

Problem:
She likes you better than (he, him).

With added words:
She likes you better than she likes him.

Correct:
She likes you better than him.

Problem:
The financial consultant is not as clever as (he, him).

With added words:
The financial consultant is not as clever as he is.

Correct:
The financial consultant is not as clever as he.

Rule 4. Technically, when a pronoun follows the verb *was, will be, is,* or *are* (that is, any form of the verb *to be*), the correct pronouns must be *I, he, she, we,* and *they.* Note the word *technically.* This is my way of hinting that this is one of the rarely observed rules.

This joke is a very old one, but it makes the point. As Saint Peter stood by the pearly gates, he heard someone approaching. "Who's there?" he called. "It is I," came the reply. "Oh," said Saint Peter, "another English teacher."

Although *It is I* is correct, most people say *It's me*, as do the French. (*C'est moi*).

However, in formal writing use the correct pronoun or, better yet, rewrite the sentence to flow more gracefully.

> No one thought that it was she who had stolen the paper clips.
>
> *or*
>
> No one thought that she was the one who had stolen the paper clips.
>
> *or*
>
> No one thought that she had stolen the paper clips.

> The next presenter will be he.
>
> *or*
>
> He will be the next presenter.

> The people who contributed the most effort were the copresidents, Belinda and she.
>
> *or*
>
> Belinda and she, the copresidents, contributed the most effort.

Answers to Chapter Challenge

Not one of the items is correct.

12   Agreement Issues

Do not sit in chair without being fully
assembled.

No one was injured in the blast, which was
attributed to a buildup of gas by one town
official.

—QUOTED BY RICHARD LEDERER IN
Anguished English

Grammar is a system in which various elements of a sentence
must be matched together correctly. When the elements are not
put together correctly, we can inadvertently create sentences that
are ungrammatical, confusing, or funny—like the ones above.

This chapter focuses on four places where errors in agreement
tend to occur—between subjects and verbs, between nouns and
pronouns, between items in a list, and between the introductory
material and the subject of a sentence (danglers).

Part 1: Subjects and Verbs

The first principle of matching is that subjects must match verbs.
That means a singular subject must be matched with a singular

verb and a plural subject must be matched with a plural verb. This sounds easy—deceptively easy.

Here is a Chapter Challenge that will make it clear how tricky matching subjects and verbs can be.

Chapter Challenge 1

See if you can choose the correct word in each of the following sentences. The answers are on page 144. Check the rules and pages provided after each item for a full explanation.

1. The instructor, as well as the administrator, (is, are) pleased with the plan. (Rule 1, Danger, page 136.)
2. Both of the administrators (is, are) mishandling the paperwork. (Rule 7, page 139.)
3. All of the items (is, are) labeled correctly. (Rule 10, page 140.)
4. She said none of the documents (is, are) in the black file cabinet. Rule 12, page 140.)
5. According to my notes, either Jane or her assistants (keeps, keep) in constant contact with the Chicago office. (Rule 13, page 141.)
6. She is one of the volunteers who (is, are) happy to work closely with our staff members. (Rule 6, page 139.)
7. This is one of the concepts that (is, are) troubling to the policy planners. (Rule 5, page 138.)
8. Each of these leaders (seems, seem) to be unaware of the seriousness of the problem. (Rule 5, page 138.)
9. Sheila and Roy said the cause for all the errors (mystifies, mystify) them. (Rule 5, Note, page 139.)
10. Smithers and he (is, are) signing the contract on behalf of the company. (Rule 1, page 136.)

Basic Rules

Rule 1. Use a plural verb when two subjects are joined by *and*. The subjects may be singular, plural, or one of each.

The manager and the supervisor are here. (two singular nouns)

The managers and the supervisors are here. (two plural nouns)

The manager and the supervisors are here. (one singular, one plural noun)

Exception:

Peanut butter and jelly is my favorite snack. (Peanut butter and jelly is considered one unit.)

Simon & Schuster is the publisher of this book. (The publishing house is considered one unit.)

DANGER: *And* is the only word that makes subjects plural. The phrases *as well as, plus, including, in addition to* after a subject do not transform a singular subject into a plural one.

Problem:

The manager, as well as the supervisor, (seem, seems) competent.

Solution:

Disregard *as well as the supervisor.*

Possibilities:

The manager seem competent.

✔ The manager seems competent.

Correct:

The manager, as well as the supervisor, seems competent.

This rule applies even if the phrase contains a plural noun.

The manager, plus the supervisors, is here.

👉 **NOTE:** These sentences are awkward; therefore, it's best to avoid these phrases and simply use *and* instead (as in Rule 1) and a plural verb.

The manager and the supervisors are here.

Rule 2: Be sure to use plural verbs with plural subjects. You can select the correct verb easily if you substitute a pronoun (*he, she, it, we,* or *they*) for the subject of the sentence.

The players (*they*) seem disgruntled.

The players and the coach (*they*) hear the crowd.

Rule 3. The verb must agree with the subject—regardless of whether the word that follows the verb is singular or plural.

Though both sentences that follow are grammatically correct, the first is more graceful.

My parents are my sole support.

My sole support is my parents.

Words to Watch Out For

Some of the following words are singular, some are plural, and some are switch-hitters. Switch-hitters can be either singular or plural. Rules 4–12 explain how to select the verb that matches these words: *a number of, another, anybody, anyone, both, each, either, every, everybody, everyone, few, many, neither, nobody, nothing, one, one of those who, one of the things that, one of the people who, others, several, the number of.*

Singular Words

Rule 4. Treat these words as singular words: *each, every, another, either, neither, one, anybody, anyone, everybody, everyone, nobody, nothing.* Use a singular verb with them.

Note: Add the word *one* after *each, every, either, neither,* and *another* to help you select the correct verb. Think of *everybody, anybody,* and *nobody* as *one body.*

> Each manager is annoyed. (Each one is annoyed.)
>
> Every candy is delicious. (Every one is delicious.)
>
> Neither candidate is qualified. (Neither one is qualified.)
>
> Everybody is amazed. (One body is amazed.)

Rule 5. If a sentence begins with *each, neither, either, one, another,* and so forth, followed by a prepositional phrase (*of the, in the*), disregard the words in the prepositional phrase and use a singular verb. Adding the word *one* will help you select the correct verb.

> Each of the topics *is* (not: are) interesting.
> (Each is interesting.)
>
> Neither of the executives *knows* (not: know) the password.
> (Neither one knows.)
>
> Either of the candidates *is* (not: are) qualified.
> (Either one is qualified.)
>
> One of Mr. Judson's ideas *is* (not: are) practical.
> (One is practical.)
>
> Another of his schemes *seems* (not: seem) destined to fail.
> (Another one seems destined to fail.)

✍ **NOTE:** The same rule applies to a plain noun. If the sentence begins with a singular noun followed by a prepositional phrase, disregard the prepositional phrase and use a singular verb.

The point in all his letters was that the company was liable for the damages.
(The point was that the company was liable for damages.)
The goal of all the employees was to find a way to increase overtime.
(The goal was to find a way to increase overtime.)

Plural Words

CAUTION: The following rule is extremely difficult!

Rule 6. After the phrase *one of those who, one of the things that, one of the people who,* **and similar phrases, use a plural verb.**

He is one of those scientists who are able to speak to nonscientists in a down-to-earth, clear manner.
This machine is one of the copiers that never break down.
This is one of the products that are being studied by Research & Development.

Rule 7. Use a plural verb with these words: *both, few, many, others, several.*

Both of the administrators are happy. (Both are happy.)
Several of the articles are useful. (Several are useful.)

Rule 8. Races, ethnic groups, and religious groups require plural verbs.

The Japanese have built indoor beaches complete with palm trees.

Rule 9. The expression *a number of* requires a plural verb. The expression *the number of* requires a singular verb.

A number of errors were detected.

The number of errors was surprisingly high.

Switch-Hitters: Words That Can Go Either Way

Rule 10. After *any, all, some, most, more,* a singular or plural verb may be needed. It depends on the sentence.

Any of the workers are capable of doing this job. (*Any* refers to the plural word *workers*. Therefore, *are* is used.)

Any worker is capable of doing this job. (*Any* refers to the singular word *worker*. Therefore, *is* is used.)

All of the workers are pleased with the product. (*All* refers to the plural word *workers*. Therefore, *are* is used.)

All of the work is done. (*All* refers to the singular word *work*. Therefore, *is* is used.)

Rule 11. Use a singular verb if a fraction refers to a singular word; use a plural verb if it refers to a plural word.

Three-fifths of the order is for our Colorado store.

One-half of the disks are missing.

Use the same system with *percent of*.

Sixty percent of the order is for our Colorado store.

Fifty percent of the disks are missing.

Rule 12. Strict grammarians insist that *none* requires a singular verb; however, in general usage *none* is singular

when it refers to a singular word, and plural when it refers
to a plural word.

> None of the *information* is available. (*Information* is a
> singular word.
>
> None of the *reports* are correct. (*Reports* is a plural word.)

🖎 **NOTE:** To emphasize the idea of singularity, use *not
one.*

Not one of the reports is correct.

Rule 13. When using *either . . . or* or *neither . . . nor,* follow
these practices.

When both subjects are singular, use a singular verb.

> Either the team leader or the secretary needs to sign the
> form. (Either one needs.)

When both subjects are plural, use a plural verb.

> Either the team leaders or the secretaries need to sign
> the form. (They need.)

**If one subject is plural and one is singular, make the verb
agree with the subject closest to the verb. The sentence
flows more smoothly when the plural word is mentioned
second.**

> Either the team leaders or the secretary signs the form.
> (The secretary signs.)
>
> Either the team leader or the secretaries sign the form.
> (The secretaries sign.)

Rule 14. When sentences start with the word *there,* keep
reading until you identify the subject. Then select the correct verb.

There is a difference between the two products. (*Difference* is the subject of the sentence.)

There are differences between the two products. (*Differences* is the subject of the sentence.)

🖎 **NOTE:** In a question, use the same system: Find the subject and then match it with either a singular or plural verb.

Incorrect:
Is there any questions?

Correct:
Are there any questions? (The subject of the sentence is *questions.)*

Similarly—

Incorrect:
Is there any reasons this report can't be completed on time?

Correct:
Are there any reasons this report can't be completed on time?

Rule 15. Some words like *committee, personnel,* and *team* can be either singular or plural.

Correct:
The committee is meeting here at 1:00 P.M. (*Committee* is thought of as one entity.)

Also correct:
The committee are not in favor of the contract terms. (Here the individual committee members are emphasized.)

Smoother:
> The committee members are not in favor of the contract terms. (Note how adding the plural word *members* improves the sentence.)

Correct:
> Our personnel is a well-trained force. (Here *personnel* is thought of as one unit.)

Also correct:
> I have heard that company personnel are unhappy with the plan. (Here *personnel* are thought of as individuals.)

Exception to the Rules

Expressions of time, money, and quantity, though plural, require a singular verb.

> Twenty-five million dollars is a lot of money.
>
> Twenty-five minutes is a long time to wait.
>
> Twenty-five and twenty-five is fifty.
>
> Twenty-five feet is the length of my driveway.

☞ **NOTE:** Generally, use the singular pronoun *it*, not *they*, for the company name.

Preferred:
> IBM has sold several divisions. It does not plan, however, to sell any more.

Acceptable
> IBM have sold several divisions. They do not plan, however, to sell any more.

Answers to Chapter Challenge 1

1. *is*—Disregard the phrase *as well as the administrator.*
2. *are*—Both . . . are mishandling.
3. *are*—*All* refers to the plural word *items*; therefore, *all . . . are labeled.*
4. *are*—*None* refers to the plural word *documents*; therefore, *none . . . are.*
5. *keep*—*Assistants* is closest to the verb; therefore, *assistants keep.*
6. *are*—*Volunteers* is plural; therefore, *volunteers are.*
7. *are*—*Concepts* is plural; therefore, *concepts are.*
8. *seems*—*Each* is a singular word; therefore, *Each* (one) *seems.*
9. *mystifies*—*The cause* is singular; therefore, *the cause* (it) *mystifies.*
10. *are*—*Smithers and he* is plural; therefore, *Smithers and he* (they) *are.*

Part 2: Nouns and Pronouns

The second principle of agreement is that nouns must match pronouns. We violate this principle often in everyday speech. We start out with a singular pronoun like *anyone, someone,* or *each,* and then throw in a *they* or a *them.*

> If *anyone* calls while I'm out, tell *them* I'll call them back. (We don't realize that *anyone* is singular and doesn't match *them,* which is plural.)

> If you love *someone,* you've got to give *them* space. (Again, *someone* is singular and does not match with *them.*)

> *Each* person should do *their* best. (Ditto!)

However, when we write we should be more precise in our word choices and make pronouns agree with the nouns they refer to. This chapter will provide four techniques for doing so.

Chapter Challenge 2

Can you locate the agreement error in each one of these sentences? The answers are on page 147. The rule noted explains each item.

1. We want each customer to feel they have been treated with care and concern. (Rule 1, below.)
2. Each employee must submit their vacation dates now. (Rule 1, below.)
3. Every team member knows their role. (Rule 1, below.)
4. Each manager should review his budget for next year. (Rule 1, below.)
5. Each staff member should be prepared to express their reactions to the new plan at the meeting next week. (Rule 1, below.)

Rule 1: If you begin a sentence with a singular word, you must maintain the singularity throughout the sentence or change the wording in one of the ways suggested below.

Here's a sentence that bothers grammarians:

I'd like everyone to take their seats.

Everyone is a singular subject. (We say *everyone* is *happy*—not *everyone are happy*.) Now, how many seats does one singular person take? One. Therefore, you cannot logically ask *each* person to take *their* seat, unless you want each person to occupy more than one seat. The singular subject, *everyone*, has been matched to the plural pronoun *their*.

How about "I'd like everyone to take his seat?" This rewrite could only be used with an all-male audience; it excludes women.

If you had an audience of both men and women, you could use any of these four approaches to be grammatically correct and nonsexist.

1. Use singular pronouns to match the singular subject.

   I'd like everyone to take his or her seat. (Clunky, but grammatically correct.)

2. Use plural words throughout.

   I'd like all the attendees to take their seats. (Grammatically correct, but a bit formal.)

3. Eliminate gender pronouns altogether.

   I'd like everyone to take a seat. (Grammatically correct and simple.)

4. Use *you* instead.

   I'd like you to take your seats. (Grammatically correct and simple.)

Let's follow the same strategy with another sentence.

Each sales rep must submit their expense vouchers by the 15th.

Problem: The subject is singular (*each sales rep*), but the pronoun is plural (*their*).
Solutions:

1. Use singular pronouns to match the singular subject.

   Each sales rep must submit his or her expense voucher by the 15th. (Grammatically correct, but clunky.)

2. Use plural words throughout.

   All sales reps must submit their expense vouchers by the 15th. (Grammatically correct and simple.)

3. Eliminate the pronouns altogether.

Each sales rep must submit an expense voucher by the 15th. (Grammatically correct and simple.)

4. Use *you* instead.

You must submit your expense vouchers by the 15th. (Grammatically correct and simple.)

Answers to Chapter Challenge 2

1. (*a*) We want each customer to feel that he or she has been treated with care and concern.
   (*b*) We want all customers to feel that they have been treated with care and concern.
   (*c*) We want you to feel you have been treated with care and concern.
2. (*a*) Each employee must submit his or her vacation dates now.
   (*b*) Each employee must submit vacation dates now.
   (*c*) Employees must submit their vacation dates now.
   (*d*) You must submit your vacation dates now.
3. (*a*) Every team member knows his or her role.
   (*b*) Team members know their roles.
   (*c*) You should know your role.
4. (*a*) Each manager should review his or her budget for next year.
   (*b*) Managers should review their budgets for next year.
   (*c*) You should review your budgets for next year.
5. (*a*) Each staff member should be prepared to express his or her reactions to the new plan at the meeting next week.
   (*b*) All staff members should be prepared to express their reactions to the new plan at the meeting next week.
   (*c*) You should be prepared to express your reactions to the new plan at the meeting next week.

Part 3: Items in a List

If John Kennedy had said:

> Ask not what your country can do for you, but about the things that can be done by you for your country.

Would anyone remember?

If Martin Luther King, Jr., had dreamed of a day when men would be known . . .

> not by the color of their skin but by their character's content . . .

Would his speech still resonate in our ears?

Or if Abraham Lincoln had prayerfully hoped that . . .

> a government of the people, by the people, and one specifically designed for those people, would long endure . . .

Would anyone recall?

Probably not. Their real quotes are memorable because each uses a type of agreement called *parallelism* in which the rhythms of the written or spoken words give special emphasis to the writer's thoughts.

Chapter Challenge 3

Each of the following is understandable; however, each could be improved by better parallelism. Identify the element in each example that breaks up the flow, and ways to overcome the problem. For an explanation see the rule accompanying each item. The answers are on page 154.

1. Please do the following:

    1. Input the new addresses
    2. Verify the zip codes
    3. The addition of client codes must be made to the customer file. (Rule 1, page 149.)

2. My goals for the weekend included:

    1. Cleaning the office
    2. Copying all the accounts receivable files
    3. To record a new voice mail message on my machine (Rule 2, page 150.)

3. Our program is

    • Easy to install
    • Easy to finance
    • Learning required is minimal.
      (Rule 2, page 150.)

4. My goals this summer are to get a new computer and then learning how to use it. (Rule 4, page 153.)
5. The assistant's responsibilities were to make travel plans, organize conferences, and training the secretary. (Rule 4, page 153.)
6. First Erica had to read what Bill had written, and then figuring out what he had meant to write. (Rule 4, page 153.)

Parallelism in Lists

Here are the rules for list making that will help you write effectively.

Rule 1. To achieve parallelism, items in lists must be either all sentences or all phrases—not a combination of both.

Note: The example below contains one sentence and two phrases. The corrected versions contains either all sentences or all phrases.

Incorrect:

The president made the following points in his presentation:

- Employee participation in safety teams has been extremely valuable. (sentence)
- No increase in accidents (phrase)
- Encourage three new teams (phrase)

Correct:

The president made the following points in his presentation:

- Employee participation in safety teams has been extremely valuable. (sentence)
- The goal for the next year is no increase in accidents. (sentence)
- Each division head is to encourage three new quality teams to form in the next six months. (sentence)

Correct:

The president made the following points in his presentation:

- The value of employee participation in safety teams (phrase)
- The goal of a zero net increase in accidents next year (phrase)
- The objective of three new quality teams to be formed by each division head in the next six months (phrase)

Rule 2. Even if all of the items in a list contain phrases, they must all also use the same type of wording.

Incorrect:

Our goals are to:

1. Improve response time (*Improve* is a simple verb.)

2. Reduce input errors (*Reduce* is a simple verb.)

3. Identifying system problems (*Identifying* is an -ing verb.)

Correct:
Our goals are to:

1. Improve response time (*Improve* is a simple verb.)

2. Reduce input errors (*Reduce* is a simple verb.)

3. Identify system problems (*Identify* is a simple verb.)

Correct:
Our goals are:

1. Improving response time (*Improving* is an *-ing* verb.)

2. Reducing input errors (*Reducing* is an *-ing* verb.)

3. Identifying system problems (*Identifying* is an *-ing* verb.)

Rule 3. The items in a list should be similar in content as well as grammar.

Grammatically, the following list is correct. Each of the three items is a sentence. Although items 1, 2, and 3 are about a similar subject, they are not as similar as they could be.

The client explained that he would not accept the shipment because:

1. The user manuals were not in three-ring binders, as stipulated in the phone conversation on July 3.

2. Some of the copy in the instructor's materials did not match the copy in the user's manual. (See attached discrepancies.)

3. The slide quality was poor.

After reading items 1 and 2, the reader knows exactly what to do. In order to make the order acceptable, he or she must put the user manuals in three-ring binders and redo the instructor's manual so it is exactly the same as the copy in the user's manual.

But what about the third item? What exactly does "slide quality was poor" mean? Is there too much information on one slide, or too many colors on each slide? Are the slides impossible to focus? Sticking together? Disintegrating?

The communication problem is that the author has matched two specific actionable statements with a general nonactionable statement.

The same problem of logic appears in this list:

> To improve the safety of our plant, the following initiatives will be taken:
>
> 1. The company will label all hazardous materials with an appropriate warning.
> 2. Safety Data Sheets will be on display in every work area.
> 3. The company is committed to providing and maintaining a safe environment for all employees.
> 4. The company will train each person who comes into contact with hazardous materials on safety procedures.
> 5. The training session will take two hours and will cover these topics: an overview of hazardous materials, safety precautions in packaging, proper handling, steps to take in an emergency.

Again, there are problems of logic here. Items 1, 2, and 4 explain steps the company will take. Item 5 goes into detail about item 4. And item 3 is simply a general statement—one that's already implied by the fact that the company is taking these actions.

A better list would look like this:

> The company is committed to providing and maintaining a safe environment for all employees. Therefore, it is taking these actions:
>
> 1. All hazardous materials will be labeled with an appropriate warning.

2. Safety Data Sheets will be on display in every work area.

3. Each employee who comes into contact with hazardous materials will attend a two-hour training session. The session will provide an overview of hazardous materials, safety precautions one should take, instructions on proper handling techniques, and steps to take in an emergency.

Parallelism in Sentences

Rule 4. Use parallelism in sentences as well as lists. Note in the examples below that each sentence really contains a list of two things. In each correct sentence, the wording is made similar so that the two items are put in sharper focus.

Incorrect:

We must teach the sales reps to use the new form and submitting the form on time is important.

Correct:

We must teach the sales reps to use the new form and submit it on time. (Both actions are expressed with the same form of the verb.)

or

We must teach the sales reps the importance of using the new form and submitting it on time. (Both actions are expressed with *-ing* words.)

Poor parallelism:

The new fax machine is easy to operate, relatively inexpensive, and it doesn't make as much noise as our old one. (Two phrases and one sentence are used to describe the fax machine.)

Good parallelism:

The new fax machine is easy to operate, relatively inexpensive, and quieter than our old one. (Three phrases are used to describe the fax machine.)

Good writers are always on the lookout for sentences that can be made clearer, more powerful, and more graceful with parallel structure. (Did you catch the parallelism in that sentence?) Isn't that sentence clearer, more powerful, and more graceful than something else I could have written, such as *Good writers are always on the lookout for sentences that can be made clearer, more powerful, and have additional gracefulness with parallel structure?*

Rule 5. Remove redundant words to improve parallelism. The improvements made below are often made in the editing process when we have a chance to look at our writing and find ways to package our ideas more concisely.

Redundant:

My boss knew how to persuade the vice president to approve the purchase and also how to obtain the funds in this year's budget.

Streamlined:

My boss knew how to persuade his boss to approve the purchase and obtain the funds in this year's budget.

Redundant:

Linda is excellent at organizing complicated tasks, and she is also superior at handling difficult people.

Streamlined:

Linda is excellent at organizing complicated tasks and handling difficult people.

Answers to Chapter Challenge 3

1. (Problem: The third item does not match.)
   Please do the following:

   1. Input the new addresses
   2. Verify the zip codes
   3. Add client codes to the customer file

2. (Problem: The third item does not match.)
   My goals for the weekend included:

   1. Cleaning the office
   2. Copying all the accounts receivable files
   3. Recording a new voice mail message on my machine

   or

   My goals this weekend are to:

   1. Clean the office
   2. Copy all the accounts receivable files
   3. Record a new voice mail message on my machine

3. (Problem: The third item does not match.)
   Our program is

   • Easy to install
   • Easy to finance
   • Easy to learn

4. (Problem: *To get* and *learning* don't match.)

   My goals this summer are to get a new computer and learn
   how to use it.

   or

   My goals this summer are getting a new computer and
   learning how to use it.

5. (Problem: *to make, organize,* and *training* don't match.)

   The assistant's responsibilities were to make travel plans,
   organize conferences, and train the secretary.

   or

   The assistant's responsibilities were making travel plans,
   organizing conferences, and training the secretary.

6. (Problem: *to read* and *figuring out* don't match.)
   First Erica had to read what Bill had written; then she had
   to figure out what he had meant to write.

Part 4: Agreement Between Introductory Material and the Subject (Danglers)

There is one more kind of agreement problem we need to discuss. This mismatch does not occur frequently, but when it does it can cause a chuckle.

Here are a few examples:

> Covered in plastic bubble wrap, I could see that the gift package was secure.

> Sitting in the last row of the bleachers, the football game was difficult to see.

> At only six months old, his mother remarried.

This chapter explains why these sentences are funny and what you can do to make them more logical. But before that, take the Chapter Challenge.

Chapter Challenge 4

Each of these sentences is illogical. Identify the reason for the problem in agreement and rewrite each sentence. The answers are on page 158. Refer to the rule after each item for an explanation of the answer.

1. After considering three fax machines, a Brother 500 was selected. (Rule 1, page 157.)
2. When analyzing the report, a statistical error was found. (Rule 1, page 157.)
3. Organized in four separate books, I found the business

directory comprehensive but difficult to use. (Rule 1, page 157.)

4. Discussing the pros and cons, the right choice became clear. (Rule 1, page 157.)
5. While listening to the music, the engine sputtered and died. (Rule 1, page 157.)

Rule 1. Make all references logical.

The sentences we've presented so far in this section are all slightly off because of what grammarians call *problems of reference*. This means that something in the sentence *refers* to something that it can't logically refer to.

Covered in plastic bubble wrap, I could see that the gift package was secure.

Covered in plastic bubble wrap seems to refer to *I*, but when you visualize someone in plastic bubble wrap, you realize that the author meant to say the gift package, not the person, was covered in plastic bubble wrap.

To make this sentence make sense, we have to make *covered in plastic bubble wrap* refer to the gift package and not the person. We can do so in a variety of ways.

I could see that the gift package covered in plastic bubble wrap was secure.

Because the gift package was covered in plastic bubble wrap, I could see that it was secure.

Covered in plastic bubble wrap, the gift package looked secure.

Let's see how we can correct the other two sentences.

Sitting in the last row of the bleachers, the football game was difficult to see.

The football game wasn't *sitting in the last row of bleachers;* the person observing the game was. Therefore, we should write:

Sitting in the last row of the bleachers, I had difficulty seeing the game.

Because I was sitting in the last row of the bleachers, I had difficulty seeing the game.

At only six months old, his mother remarried.

At only six months old can't logically refer to the mother's age. It refers to someone else, but the someone else it refers to is not in the sentence. The sentence would make more sense if it said:

When he was only six months old, his mother remarried.

His mother remarried when he was only six months old.

The phrases we've pointed out are called dangling phrases because they don't have anything in the original sentences to attach themselves to: They just dangle. To correct these sentences we added the missing people or things.

Answers to Chapter Challenge 4

The remedy in all cases is to add the missing people or things. We've made up names to make the sentences logical and grammatically correct.

1. (Problem: The fax machine can't consider anything.)

   After considering three fax machines, Bob selected the Brother 500.

   After Bob considered the three fax machines, he selected a Brother 500.

2. (Problem: A statistical error can't analyze.)

   When Cheryl analyzed the report, she found a statistical error.

   When the report was analyzed, Cheryl found a statistical error.

   Cheryl found a statistical error when she was analyzing the report.

3. (Problem: I am not organized in four separate books.)

Organized in four separate books, the business directory was comprehensive but difficult to use.

I found the business directory comprehensive but difficult to use because it was organized in four separate books.

I found the business directory, which was organized in four separate books, comprehensive but difficult to use.

4. (Problem: The right choice did not discuss.)

After we discussed the pros and cons, the right choice became clear.

The right choice became clear after we discussed the pros and cons.

5. (Problem: The engine did not listen to the music.)

As we listened to the music, the engine sputtered and died.

The engine sputtered and died as we listened to the music.

Part Five

Mastering Business Writing

13 "Did You Get My Memo?"

> There's nothing to writing. All you do is sit down at a typewriter and open a vein.
>
> —RED SMITH

You spend most of the morning working on an important memo. You fuss over the words, read it over, and with a sigh of relief, send it out.

And then—nothing. Your phone doesn't ring. Nobody comes to your office. No memo comes to your desk.

Finally, you can't stand it anymore. So you call up and ask, "Did you get my memo?" The fumbling reply tells you that he or she got the piece of paper you sent, but not the message.

Alas! Message sent is not necessarily message received.

If you want somebody's share of mind, you've got to *earn* it— by applying these principles.

1. Bottoms up!

When you were in school, you were taught how to write essays. Begin with an introduction, then write the body, then the conclusion. Effective business writing is the opposite of essay writing. You start with the conclusion and then move into the body, the details. It's more like a newspaper article, with the *who, what, when, where,* and *how* told first and the details later.

To show you exactly how this works, let's look at two memos: the first one in the typical essay format and the second one in the "bottoms up" format. I've indicated in brackets how the reader might react to each line.

Memo 1

To: Tom Olson
           Export Regulation Manager—Denmark
From: Headquarters Audit Group
Subject: U.S. Export Regulations Audit

Audit teams from the World Trade Export Regulation Office will be visiting a number of countries during June. [*Are they coming here?*] These audits will cover all areas of export compliance, including the Distribution License Internal Control Program, shipments of individual license and DES commodities, technical data requirements and procedures. [*OK, but are they coming here?*]

The visit to Denmark is planned for June 6–11 and the team members are Ms. Linda Jones and Mr. Robert Halley. [*They are coming. Let me mark my calendar.*] We would like you to make meeting arrangements and hotel reservations. The team will also need a guest ID on your PROFS system and secretarial assistance for their final audit report. [*I'll get Carol to do this.*]

If you have any questions or comments, I can be reached at (202) 833-7095.

Memo 2

To:	Tom Olson
	Export Regulation Manager—Denmark
From:	Headquarters Audit Group
Subject:	U.S. Export Regulations Audit

On June 6–11, an audit team made up of Ms. Linda Jones and Mr. Robert Halley will be visiting Denmark as part of our European audits. [*They're coming. Let me mark my calendar.*] Their audit will cover all areas of export compliance, including the Distribution License Internal Control Program, shipments of individual license and DES commodities, technical data requirements and procedures. [*OK.*]

We would like you to make meeting arrangements and hotel reservations for Ms. Jones and Mr. Halley. The team will need guest ID on your PROFS system and secretarial assistance for their final audit. [*I'll get Carol to do this.*]

If you have any questions, I can be reached at (202) 833-7095.

As you can see, the memo format gets the point across immediately. By eliminating the introduction, we created a shorter, more targeted piece of writing.

2. Don't zigzag.

Put all related thoughts together in paragraphs or in lists. Otherwise, you look disorganized and unprofessional. All we've done below is repackage the writing. But notice how much more intelligent the writer of the revised memo looks than the writer of the original one. (By the way, both memos were written by the same person!)

Original

To: Tom Johnson
Subject: Professional Development Day

As of today we have received more than 200 reservations for our professional development day. Naturally, we are extremely pleased with this response.

Karen Goodwell has generously offered to let us use the audiovisual equipment at her company for the entire day, so that we can use overheads, easels, and film projectors at no additional cost. She will contact the speakers and get a list of their audiovisual needs.

Please arrange to have the keynote speaker taped. Ms. Famous will be speaking from 1:00 P.M. to 3:00 P.M.

I will provide blue 3-ring binders for each participant. (They can accommodate all the course materials for the day.)

Please inform all the committee people that each committee person is entitled to bring *one guest*. No exceptions will be made!

One other point, please send me a floor plan of the exhibit area. I want to be sure we don't stick anyone in a dark corner.

I think we will have a great professional day if we keep on working together and coordinating all the planning steps. Thanks for all the work you've done.

Revised

To: Tom Johnson
Subject: Professional Development Day

As of today we have received more than 200 reservations for our professional development day. Naturally, we are extremely pleased with this response.

I would like to ask your assistance on three items:

- Arrange to have the keynote speaker, Ms. Famous, taped. She will be speaking from 1:00 to 3:00 P.M.

- Tell all the committee people that each committee person is entitled to bring *one* guest. No exceptions will be made.

- Finally, please send me a floor plan of the exhibit area. I want to be sure we don't stick anyone in a dark corner.

I'm pleased to tell you that Karen Goodwell has generously offered to let us use the audiovisual equipment at her company for the entire day, so we can use overheads, easels, and film projectors at no additional cost. She will contact the speakers and get a list of their audiovisual needs.

I will provide blue 3-ring binders for each participant. They can hold all the course materials for the day.

I think we will have a great professional day if we keep on working together and coordinating all the steps.

Thanks for all the work you've done.

3. Avoid killer sentences.

Your sentences should not exceed 24 words: that's about 2½ typewritten lines. (Of course, there will be exceptions.) Before you print a memo, read it aloud. If you find that you run out of breath before you get to the end of your sentences, go back and edit: Your sentences are too long. (By the way, the most readable material contains a variety of long, medium, and short sentences. Note that this paragraph contains eight sentences of various lengths. Here's how many words are in each sentence of this paragraph: 12, 6, 8, 27, 16, 10, 19, 6. Variety helps keep the writing interesting.)

4. Avoid killer paragraphs.

Have you ever picked up a one-page memo that consists of two paragraphs? One occupies most of the page, the other one line. Ugh!

How many sentences should be in a paragraph depends on two things: looks and logic.

Newspaper paragraphs usually contain only two or three sentences, but books contain many more. Why? Our eye is used to a certain amount of white space relative to the page. If you use too many large paragraphs, the reader is overwhelmed by material and will not want to read it.

But paragraphing is more than starting a new paragraph just because it would be nice to give the reader some white space. You must look for the logical place to start a new paragraph, the place where there's a change in the thought. So if you've produced a killer paragraph, reread it and find the place where a new paragraph could begin.

5. Be goal oriented.

Each memo should be designed to accomplish a work purpose: to tell someone something (transfer information), to tell someone to do something (stimulate action), or to change someone's idea (persuade).

Do not sit down to write and say to yourself, "I've got to write a memo about the problem with our inventory system." Rather, say, "I've got to write to Bob and get him to put new stickers on the vats in Warehouse A." Not "I've got to write about the expense report," but "I've got to explain the new expense report system to the field so they can get their reports in faster."

Think more about the *object* of your writing than the *subject* of your writing.

6. Stress benefits.

When introducing a new system, a new procedure, or a new policy, think about the benefits to your readers. Will it help them get something done faster, with fewer errors, with greater ease, at less cost? If so, put those benefits in the first paragraph.

Here are the original and rewrite about a new procedure for ordering office repairs and equipment.

Original:

Building Services has eliminated the requirement to submit a written Facilities Services Request to rearrange or repair office furniture. These requests can now be expedited by phone. This should result in a shorter period between the initiation of a request and the provision of the service requested.

Revised:

Building Services has changed its procedures so that you can get faster service. You can now phone in requests to rearrange or repair furniture, rather than fill out and submit a Facilities Service Request.

But what, you ask, if there are no benefits? What if your message creates nothing but more work for the reader?

My suggestion: Admit it. Explain why this new action is required, tell the reader how much work you estimate is involved. Don't pretend it's a trifle if it's not. You might write something like this:

Administration requires that we submit a 402K Form for each part-time employee. This process should take approximately 4–6 minutes per employee. Please complete the form and return it to Mark Simons by August 1.

7. Use a stapler.

I once knew a fellow whose job entailed going to several computer conferences each year and writing up a review for his boss. His write-ups were clear, interesting, and detailed, about five to seven pages long. I was impressed. When I asked him how long it took him to write these reports, he said about five hours. He explained that he didn't have time to do it at work, so he did it at home on the weekends. In fact, he had one to write this weekend. He'd rather play golf, he said, but the conference report was overdue, and his boss needed it on Monday.

I looked again at the report. Did his boss really want a recap of each seminar, starting with the first one at 9:00 A.M. Monday and ending with the last one at 4:00 P.M. on Wednesday? What, in fact, was the purpose of the report? To prove that he actually went to the conference and sat through each seminar, or to communicate what was new and useful to the company?

I suggested a new system of writing reports. Start with this objective: to tell your boss three things you learned or saw at the conference that have potential for improving your group's work. Take a paragraph to explain each one. Show how the new technology or the concept might work in the company. List potential benefits and problems. Suggest next steps. If you want permission to explore one area further, ask for it.

Then get a stapler. Staple the conference brochure that contains a recap of each seminar.

Voilà! Twice as good, one-sixteenth as much work, and much more gratifying for writer and reader. The boss was delighted to see, up front, the return on his investment.

8. Focus on three things.

Sometimes when we sit down to write monthly activity reports, trip reports, recaps of meetings, we are overwhelmed by detail. We don't know where to start.

Help organize your thoughts by asking yourself, "What are the three main points I want to get across? What are the three main ideas that this person needs to know?"

But, you say, what if there are 11 main points you want to communicate? I hate to be rude, but I don't believe you. There are never 11 *main* points, although there may be 11 points. Most likely these points will fit into three main points—four at the most.

Here's a list of 11 features in a building that a company would like to purchase. Can we make this into a list of three and not lose anything? Of course we can. And in doing so, we actually give our writing more impact.

Original:
The new building must have these characteristics:

1. 25,000 to 30,000 square feet
2. A fireproof vault of about 1,000 square feet
3. Cost no more than $1,000,000 for the first five years
4. A loading dock
5. No more than four stories high
6. Sublease clause
7. New Jersey, Connecticut, or New York State
8. Good access to major highways
9. Adequate space for a data center of 8,000 square feet
10. A 10-to-20-year year lease
11. Within 50 miles of a major airport

Revised—organized in three categories:
The new building must have these characteristics:

Standard Features

- 25,000 to 30,000 square feet
- A fireproof vault of about 1,000 square feet

- A loading dock
- No more than four stories
- Adequate space for an 8,000 square feet data center

Cost/Lease Provisions

- Cost no more than $1,000,000 for the first five years
- Sublease clause
- 10-to-20-year term

Location

- New Jersey, Connecticut, or New York State
- Within 50 miles of a major airport
- Accessible to major highways

If you look at your list of 11 or 23 or 108 points, issues, or items, and you don't see a way to reduce them into under three categories, you can still group them into two categories: Major Points and Minor Points, Primary Considerations and Secondary Considerations, and so forth. By sorting information into categories, we instantly improve our power to communicate.

9. Keep your eye on the reader.

I was talking about letter writing with a secretary who works in the corporate loan department of a major bank. She told me that although her letters to clients explained exactly which documents the bank needed, who had to sign each document, which ones had to be notarized, which ones had to have the corporate seal affixed, and so on, she rarely, if ever, got back the forms signed by the right people in the right place. People, she felt, were just too dumb or sloppy or whatever to follow her directions.

I looked at her letter requesting the loan documents. It looked beautiful—clearly worded, good paragraphing, nice margins. Each document was listed with clear directions on how to fill it out.

What was the problem? Her letter was organized, but not for the needs of the reader—the secretary at the company who had to get all the documents signed and sealed. Some documents had to be forwarded to the treasurer for signature, some to the president, and some to all the officers. Some had to have the corporate seal affixed, and some didn't. Getting the paperwork done correctly meant checking the forms to make sure each officer had filled out the correct part: not an impossible job, but a complicated one.

I asked the secretary at the bank to pretend she was the receiving secretary, the one at the company applying for the loan. How would she go about getting the paperwork done? "Easy," she said. "I'd simply make a list of who signs what and work from that list."

With that insight, she rewrote her letter. It now listed each officer and the documents he or she had to sign. Her letter looked, in part, like this:

Treasurer must sign:

- Form 21a, page 3, bottom
- Form 1007L—page 2 back and front
- State Insurance Certificate—Side A, bottom left

This simple change resulted in considerably improved paper-work submissions. (By the way, the bank secretary got even savvier. She bought different colors of Post-It® flags and gave each officer a color. Her new letter said:

Please have each corporate officer sign the enclosed documents at the appropriate color flag:

Treasurer—green flag

President—red flag

Now, that involves sticking on a lot of flags, but the secretary found that she actually saved time in the end since she now had almost 100 percent correct responses.

Before you write, take a few moments to think about the

reader and his or her needs; you will find the best way to organize your writing.

10. Write less, say more.

You can become a more efficient writer by keeping two goals in mind: Write only what is necessary and strive to write that in the most compact way possible. Write, "We need to *streamline* that process," rather than, "We need to *determine a system that will result in the fewest steps possible to process the application.*" Write, "After carefully considering the options, I have decided to continue working with the vendor on the design," rather than, "After careful consideration of all the options you presented at our meeting last week, a determination has been made that we should continue working with the vendor on the design."

Take a look at your last memo and challenge yourself: How could I have written the same thing in half the words? (That's the technique Ben Franklin developed to make himself an effective writer.) Refer to the list of business verbs on page 235; they are simple action words that you'll find useful.

11. Shun the *-tion*.

One thing that leads to a heavy tone is the habit of using words that end in *-tion*.

> Upon an evaluation of the errors, a determination was made that the production of errors was caused by unauthorized manipulation of the formula.

Huh?

> After we studied the errors, we determined that they were caused by a chemist who made unauthorized changes in the formula.

Oh!

Overuse of *-tion* coupled with an overreliance on the passive voice (*a determination was made by us* versus *we determined*) is a deadly combination.

12. Clarity, not just brevity, is the goal.

Although we stress that the fewer words, the better, we don't mean to imply that brevity is the sole criterion of good business writing. Clarity is. Getting the complete message to the right person is. Therefore, always add words if they add clarity.

"I need your help on this project" may not be as good as "Please review the list of procedures on page 8 of the enclosed report and delete any that are no longer in use. I must have your edited list on my desk on the 19th."

"The meeting was a great success!" may be a great way to recap a meeting. Or it may be better to list the three major things that were accomplished. It all depends on the situation and the reader.

13. Never be a bore.

Don't write unless you have something new to communicate or can find a new way to communicate something old. Memos and speeches that begin by telling people what they already know produce yawns. How many times have we read a sentence like this: *Quality is essential in today's competitive marketplace?* Wouldn't it be better to tell us about how one team worked on one quality initiative and succeeded or failed and what we can learn from their success or failure? How many times have we been told, *It is critical that we maximize our resources?* Wouldn't it be more helpful if we learned how, when, and where people have maximized their resources?

Write to people in your own voice; don't lecture from a podium in someone else's.

14. Test Market your writing.

To be sure that message sent is message received, test market critical memos before you send them. Be sure that the person who test reads your work has similar knowledge of, and attitude toward, the issues raised in the memo as the ultimate reader.

Ask your surrogate readers to let you know immediately when they find themselves getting confused—even momentarily confused. A confused reader means there are trouble spots in your memo. You will need to add information, choose a better word, or simplify the sentence structure to remove those problems.

Once you've ensured that your writing is clear, ask your surrogate reader these questions:

1. Was the memo convincing?
2. What could have been added to make it more convincing?
3. What objections might someone raise after reading the memo?

Listen carefully to the feedback and make any necessary changes.

14 Answers to Your Questions on Letter Writing

> Excuse me for not answering your letter sooner, but I've been so busy not answering letters that I couldn't get around to not answering yours in time.
>
> —GROUCHO MARX

Despite the use of faxes and E-mail, letters continue to be an important part of business communication. After all, the signature on a fax is clearly, well, a facsimile of the real thing, and E-mail has a slapdash look. Letters *are* the real thing, and when done well they communicate the care, concern, and professionalism of the writer for the reader.

Here are answers to questions I am often asked about letter writing.

1. How long should a letter be?

The answer depends on your purpose. Direct marketers, whose junk mail fills our mailboxes, have documented that multipage letters with lots of enclosures sell better than one-page letters.

But a businessperson is more likely to read a one-page letter than a two- or three-page one.

If you draft a three- or four-page business letter and want to be sure it gets read, write a one-page letter listing the key points and then add enclosures that spell out the details. For example, if you wish to explain three options the client has for solving a technical problem, don't write a four-page letter in which you fully explain option one, option two, and then option three. It's much more effective and professional to write a cover letter that highlights the three options followed by a three-page enclosure that spells out the details. This system increases your chances of producing letters that impress your reader and get results.

2. What if my letter is too short?

Have you ever written a one-paragraph business letter and then struggled to find something else to say because you thought your letter looked too skimpy? This is a mistake. Instead of adding unimportant or redundant information, simply increase the margins—top, bottom, and especially left and right—so that your letter looks centered on the page. That will ensure that your letter looks professional and complete.

However, there are a few cases in which a very short letter is not appropriate. Thank-you letters are good examples. If you are asked to write thank-you letters to speakers who made presentations at a conference, don't just write, "Thank you for speaking to our sales force at our recent conference. Your presentation was extremely informative and interesting. Sincerely. . . ."

This is too short, too dull, and too predictable. It sounds like an all-purpose thank-you letter that you've pulled out of your files.

Personalize it. Individualize it. Tell your speaker something he or she said that was particularly useful and memorable.

For example, you might say:

Thank you for giving our sales force such a vivid picture of the new incentive program. You managed to make this rather complicated plan understandable! The hand-outs with examples enabled us to see just how commissions will be calculated.

We appreciate your clear explanations and helpful tips.

Sincerely,

This letter is only four sentences, but it shows the speaker that someone heard and appreciated the talk.

3. Do you always put a colon after the *Dear So-and-So* in a business letter?

No. Until recently, salutations (the *Dear So-and-So* line) always consisted of a *Dear Mr.* or *Ms. Smith* followed by a colon. Today, the rules are more relaxed. If you are on a first-name basis with the reader, you may write *Dear Robert:*—or even *Dear Robert,* if you are writing a very informal note. But do not say *Dear Robert* unless you sign your first name as well. (It's rude to address someone more informally than you sign yourself.) If you sign your first name, be sure your full name is typed below your signature.

Some writers use this tack. They type *Dear Mr. Smith* but then cross that out and handwrite *Robert.* This will certainly draw the reader's attention to the fact that you feel you have both a personal and a business relationship.

Caution

Although letter writing has gotten more informal, do not address people you do not know with a first name. Many executives have told me that they resent this practice.

4. What's the best font for a letter?

The word *font* refers to typeface (for example, Times Roman), typestyle (roman, italic, bold, bold italic), and size. The font that's easiest to read is Times Roman (*not* Helvetica) 12-point. If you reduce the size to 11-point or even further, you reduce the chances of your letter being read promptly. If you want to fit your letter on one page without using a hard-to-read point size, read the answer to Question 1.

5. How many fonts can I use in one letter or document?

One is best. You may want to highlight headings by using a font 2 points larger than the regular type, and you may want to bold those headings, or occasionally italicize a key phrase. But don't use three or four different fonts plus boldface type and italics. A busy letter turns off rather than attracts readers in the business world.

6. What if I don't know the name of the person I'm writing to?

If you don't know someone's name, don't address the person as *Dear Sir or Madam.* Use the reader's job title or other descriptive term.

Correct:
> Dear Accounts Payable Personnel, Dear Customer, Dear Employee, Dear Taxpayer

Rapidly becoming obsolete:
> Dear Sir or Madam

7. What if I know the name but can't tell whether it's a man or woman's name?

Write *Dear Leslie Smith* or *Dear Tony Jones*. Better yet, call the person's organization and ask, "I'm addressing a letter to Leslie Smith. Is that Mr. or Ms.?"

8. Should I use *Ms.* instead of *Mrs.* or *Miss*?

Yes, unless a woman signs her name or refers to herself as *Mrs.* or *Miss.*

9. If I am writing to two people at the same company, how do I handle the inside address and the salutations?

List the individuals in order of position:

> Mr. Robert Jones, Senior Vice President
>
> Ms. Ellen Smith, Vice President
>
> Affiliated Resources
>
> 601 East 57th Street
>
> New York, New York 10022

The salutation for two men:

> Dear Mr. Smith and Mr. Jones:
>
> Dear Messrs. Smith and Jones:

The salutation for one man and one woman:

> Dear Mr. Smith and Ms. Jones:

The salutation for two women:

> Dear Ms. Smith and Ms. Jones:

10. How do I close the letter?

Sincerely, Sincerely yours, Cordially, Cordially yours are the most pop-ular closes. *Very truly yours* and *Respectfully yours* are used in formal situations. Some writers have replaced these with the phrase *With warm regards* or just *Regards*.

The tradition of writing *Dear So-and-So* and *Sincerely yours* seems odd in our casual business atmosphere. We do not begin or end conversations with these terms and we don't mean them when we write them. In the next decade, I am sure that we will create more up-to-date ways of starting and ending letters, though I hope it's not "Have a nice day!"

11. What's the best cc policy?

Be cautious in your use of cc's. Whether or not to cc your boss, your subordinate, your team members is a question you should consider carefully. In general, people like to feel that a letter is between two people, not twenty. However, sometimes adding a cc shows the reader that you have taken action by referring the matter to an important person in your organization.

12. What's the best order for listing the cc's?

Some companies list people in order of seniority, others simply in alphabetical order. The latter is easier and better.

15 Netiquette—E-Mail Etiquette

> To err is human but to really foul things up requires a computer.
>
> —*Farmers Almanac,* 1978

E-mail has become *the* method of communication in corporate life. It is so easy to use that no one has, as yet, complained of writer's block while using E-mail. This is both wonderful and awful for communication—wonderful in that people share ideas more frequently with people in the next office and across the world than they did when memo and letter writing were the only options, awful in that E-mail is often verbose, often hard to read, and sometimes impolite. Confidentiality is a problem. Even though you may have erased an E-mail, there is no guarantee that it does not lurk in some system backup file, ready to surface. And of course, there are stories about individuals who have written confidential, even intimate, E-mail to a co-worker, only to discover that through the slip of a finger, their E-mail has been sent to the entire distribution list.

The sheer user friendliness of E-mail causes people to write too much, at too great length, to too many people. This has resulted in a new corporate anxiety: dread of that little bleep that says another E-mail has arrived. Here are some rules to improve E-mail quality.

1. Don't get sloppy.

Because E-mail is so user friendly, people revert to stream-of-consciousness writing. Sometimes when I look at my E-mail, I swear my correspondents are e. e. cummings or James Joyce. Unpunctuated writing is hard to read. It demonstrates a lack of concern for the reader.

Observe the basics. DON'T USE ALL CAPITAL LETTERS. IT'S ANNOYING. don't use all small letters. ditto. Use punctuation. Start a new paragraph when the thought changes course. Proofread your E-mail before you hit the "send" key.

2. Beautify it.

E-mail is ugly.

Savvy E-mail users have learned to format their E-mail to make it more visually appealing. Learn how to make margins and indent for lists. If possible, change the default so the distribution list will appear at the *end*, not the beginning, of the E-mail. (How many times have you scrolled over two screens of a distribution list to find this E-mail: "The meeting next week has been moved to RoomB"? Once in a while, cc yourself so you see how your memos look and read.

3. Control the clutter.

It started out as a nice idea—attaching the prior correspondence so the reader could understand the background of the issue you are writing about. But if readers have to go through four screens of previous E-mails and piece together everything that's happened to date, they won't have much patience or energy for your E-mail.

Summarize the events or discussions leading up to your message. Say, "Here's a recap," and follow with a list of major events or issues so far. Then you can also attach the actual prior notes after your E-mail for reference.

4. When you sit down to type, don't.

The blessing of E-mail is that it's quick and informal. The curse of E-mail is that it's quick and informal. As a result, E-mailers tend to ramble. Figure out, *before you begin,* what you want to say and how you want to have it sound to that reader. Then, and only then, put your hands on the keyboard. Don't fill up two screens when one will do the job.

5. Be appropriate.

E-mail is not the medium for discussing a performance issue with a subordinate or influencing a superior to take a new course of action. (This is better done person to person or on paper.) E-mail is best for transferring information or sharing hunches, for mundane tasks such as filling out forms or making a lunch date. If you're not sure E-mail is the right medium for your message, don't use it.

6. Starting off and signing off

Clearly, *Dear So-and-So* is too formal for E-mail. Many people just begin writing their message. Some start with "Hello" or the person's first name. ("Yo" is probably too casual.)

You can end with just your name. Some people add a *&* on a line by itself. This means "I look forward to hearing from you."

7. Watch your language.

E-mail is not the place for pejorative statements about the organization's products or people, or romantic notes to a fellow employee. Not long ago *The Wall Street Journal* told the story of a couple whose Monday morning E-mail about the weekend they had spent together appeared on the screen of every single employee in the organization. Before you hit the send key, make sure you would not be embarrassed if your E-mail appeared on everyone's screen. Remember the caveat of Bill Moroney, the executive director of the Electronic Mail Association, "The PC provides an *illusion* of privacy."

8. Be responsive.

If you don't have time to respond to an E-mail in full, at least E-mail the writer and let him or her know when you will be able to respond. You probably have a facility on your system that allows you to send an automatic acknowledgement that says, "I've received your E-mail, but I can't respond just now. I will get back to you at the end of the month."

If you will be away, put a note on your system so that people won't think they are being ignored. Let them know whom to contact in your absence. And of course, remember to shut off that feature when you return.

9. E-Mail Lingo

Over the past few years, unique E-mail symbols and terms have been created. If you see any of these in your E-mail, here's what they mean. The first three will be better understood if you turn the page so you can see the faces.

1. :-)   Joke
2. ;-)   A wink—just kidding!
3. :-(A grimace
4. &   I look forward to hearing from you.
5. g   Grin

6. ROF,L   Rolling on floor, laughing
7. OIC   Oh, I see.
8. BTW   By the way
9. IMHO   In my humble opinion

To flame—to express oreself by using insulting or provocative language
To engage in flame wars—self-explanatory

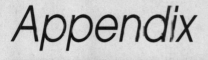

Appendix

Troublesome Words
and Phrases

"Whom are you?" he said, for he had been
to night school.

This section includes words that present spelling problems
(*accept/except, all together/altogether*), usage problems (*affect/effect;
assure/ensure/insure*) and grammar problems (*he felt bad* versus *he
felt badly, who* versus *whom*).

You will find all the items your tenth-grade English teacher
warned you about, plus some new ones.

A, an

Use *an* before words that begin with a vowel sound.

He is *an* ill-informed person.

In the next example, even though *u* is a vowel, it is sounded
like the letter *y*, a consonant, and thus does not take the word *an*
before it.

The secretary developed *a* unit on vacation policy for
the new handbook.

Some people say *an historic occasion;* however, *a historic occasion* is correct because the *h* is pronounced.

Accept, except

Accept and *except* are two different words and are to be pronounced differently.
   Accept (AK-cept′): to receive.

> Please *accept* this gift as our thanks for your help.

Except (X-cept′): This is related to the word *exception*.

> I'll make an *exception* in your case.

> Everyone *except* Jane knows the password.

Advice, advise

Advise is what you do. *Advice* is what you get.

> I *advised* Susan to get a lawyer who could give her good *advice* about her divorce.

Affect, Effect

Use *affect* when you can substitute the phrase *do something to, did something to, will do something to,* and so forth in the sentence. (*Affect* is a verb.)

> My mother *affects* my nerves.
> My mother *does something to* my nerves.

> The long commute *affected* his disposition.
> The long commute *did something to* his disposition.

> The early retirement offer will not *affect* her.
> The early retirement offer will not *do something to* her.

Use *effect* when you can substitute the word *result* in the sentence. (*Effect* is a noun.)

The *effect* of the budget cuts was obvious: production plummeted.

The *result* of the budget cuts was obvious: production plummeted.

His angry speech had no *effect* on me.
His angry speech had no *result* on me.

Their decision will have no *effect* on us.
Their decision will have no *result* on us.

Occasionally (and here's the hard part) *effect* is used as a verb, to mean *to create* rather than *to do something to.*

The transaction was *effected* (*created,* not: *done something to*) on March 1.

All ready, already

All ready refers to being *fully prepared.*

The three packages were *all ready* for mailing.

Already means *previously.*

He had *already* done the work.

All right, alright

Alright is incorrect. (Some dictionaries note that *alright* is acceptable in informal writing, but it's best not to use it.) The correct phrase is *all right.*

It's *all right* (not: *alright*) with me.

All together, altogether

All together means *gathered in a group.*

We were *all together* for the high school reunion.

Altogether means *entirely*.

> Ruth was not *altogether* pleased with the format of the quarterly report.

Allusion, illusion

Allusion is a reference to something.

> The CEO made an *allusion* to how much profits would increase.

An *illusion* is a false dream or an exaggerated, unrealistic idea.

> The company has the *illusion* that the next quarter will be profitable.

Alot

Always incorrect. Use the two words *a lot* instead. (*A lot* should be used only in informal writing. Avoid using it in academic or business writing.)

Informal:
> He produced a lot of evidence.

Formal:
> He produced a good deal of evidence.

a.m., p.m. (or A.M., P.M.)

Use the abbreviation only with numbers.

> I'll see you at 8:30 A.M.

> I'll see you in the *morning*.

Avoid this expression:

> I'll see you in the *a.m.*

Amount, number

Amount refers to things that cannot be counted, *number* to things that can.

> A large *number* (not: *amount*) of errors were found in the document.

And/or

This term should only be used for legal matters.

Anxious, eager

Anxious is related to the word *anxiety* and thus refers to fearful anticipation.

> I was *anxious* about the upcoming exam.

Eager refers to happy anticipation.

> I was *eager* to see the new movie.

This distinction is not often observed in everyday speech.

Anywheres, everywheres, nowheres, anyways

These words are not correct. Remove the *s* of each one.

> I couldn't find it *anywhere* (not: *anywheres*).

Appraise, apprise

Appraise means to *determine a value of*.

> We *appraised* my mother's diamond.

Apprise is to *inform*.

> We will *apprise* you of any progress.
>
> We will keep you *apprised* of developments.

As

Do not use *as* when you mean *because* . . .

> *Because* (not: *As*) the meeting started late, we canceled the introductory speeches.

or when you mean *whether*.

> I didn't know *whether* (not: *as*) I could go.

As per

The Latin word *per* means *for every*. For unknown reasons, the expression *per your letter* meaning *in reference to your letter* has become common in business writing. This usage is frowned upon because it is a mistranslation of the word *per*. Even more frowned upon is the expression *as per*.

Incorrect:

> *As per* your letter, we are researching your file. (This means *as for every your letter* or *as in reference to your letter*—clearly not what the reader intended.)

Frowned upon:

> *Per* your letter, we are researching your file.

More user friendly:

> As you requested in your letter, we are researching your file.

As to

Frowned upon:
> I questioned him *as to* his reasons.

Correct:
> I questioned him *about* his reasons.

Assure, ensure, insure

This is a complicated one. All three words mean to guarantee or make certain. Use *assure,* not *ensure* or *insure,* when people, not things, are involved.

> He *assured* me the work would be done by tomorrow morning (not: *ensured* or *insured*).

Use *ensure, insure,* or *assure* when things are involved.

Preferred:
> He worked hard to *ensure* (or: *insure*) the program's success.

Acceptable:
> He worked hard to assure the program's success.

Use *insure* when insurance is involved.

> She *insured* her car for the maximum amount (not: *assured* or *ensured*).

At

At is sometimes redundant.

Incorrect:
> Where's he *at?*

Correct:
> Where is he?

At this point in time

Wordy. Use *now* instead.

Bad, badly

Which is correct?

> Robert sings *bad*.
>
> *or*
>
> Robert sings *badly*.

The correct answer is *Robert sings badly*.

To understand why this is the correct choice, you must understand these three points:

Point 1: *Bad* describes people or things.

> One *bad* apple spoils the barrel.
>
> They used a *bad* photo on my license.

Point 2: *Badly* describes how someone or something *does* an action. It answers the question *how*.

> He plays baseball *badly*. (*How* does he play? Badly.)
>
> He reacts *badly* to criticism. (*How* does he react? Badly.)

Therefore, the correct answer is:

> Robert sings *badly*. (He does something—sings—poorly.)

Similarly:

> This software works *badly* on this system.
>
> He handled the customer *badly*.

Point 3: After any form of the verbs *to be, to feel, to smell,* or *to taste,* the correct choice is *bad*.

> This is a *bad* piece of software.
>
> Robert is *bad*.
>
> Robert feels *bad* (not: *badly*).
>
> Robert smells *bad* (not: *badly*). This means he does not shower frequently.
>
> The hamburger tastes *bad* (not: *badly*).

Questions:

1. Is it ever correct to say *Robert smells badly?*
   Possibly. If Ralph had wanted to get a job as a perfume tester but was rejected because his nose wasn't sensitive enough to sniff the perfumes, we'd use *badly* because *badly* refers to how he did the smelling—how he did something.

   Ralph smelled *badly;* therefore, he was unable to get the job of perfume tester.

(Now honestly, how often will you need to say that?)

2. What about *Robert felt badly?* Isn't that ever correct?
   Again, the only way that sentence is grammatically correct is if you want to say that Robert has a disease that makes him unable to feel things.

   Robert feels badly. Unfortunately, he has diabetes, and as a result, the nerve endings in his fingers do not sense textures.

Therefore, say and write *he feels bad* when you want to say a person feels sad or is sick.

For a similar usage issue, see *Good, well.*

Because, due to

Careful writers use *because,* not *due to,* in introductory phrases and *due to* after a form of the verb *to be* (*is, was, will be,* and so forth).

> *Because of* (not: *Due to*) the stock increase, the officers made a bundle.
>
> *but*
>
> Her success is *due to* (not: *because of*) hard work, not good luck.

However, *due to* is so commonly used as an introductory phrase that it will probably gain acceptance. By the way, it is perfectly fine to start a sentence with *because* (see page 16).

Being as, being that

Being as or *being that* is a nonstandard expression.

> *Because* I was late, I took a shortcut. (NOT *Being as* I was late, I took a shortcut.)

Between, among

Use *between* when referring to two entities.

> The battle was *between* the conservatives and the liberals.

Use *among* when referring to three or more entities.

> There was a disagreement *among* the five panelists.

Exception: Use *between* if something is being physically divided.

> The tip was divided *between* the waiter, the hostess, and the busboy.

Bi- and semi-

Words that have the *bi-* prefix are potentially ambiguous. The dictionary says *biweekly* means (1) occurring every two weeks, (2) occurring twice a week. How often then does a biweekly meeting take place?

To avoid these kinds of questions, avoid using *bi-* and instead use the phrase *every two weeks* or *twice a week,* or the prefix *semi-*, meaning *twice every.* (A semiannual premium is paid twice a year.)

Both alike, both equal

Do not use these terms, because they are redundant. Use just *alike* or *equal.*

> The identical cousins were *alike* (not: *both alike*) in so many ways.

> The two computers were *equal* (not: *both equal*) in price.

Brake, break

Break: to *shatter* or *split.*

> Don't *break* your perfect record.

Brake: to *apply the brake.*

> I *brake* for deer.

Bring, take

Bring refers to motion toward the speaker.

> Please *bring* the file to me.

Take refers to motion away from the speaker.

> *Take* the book to Ms. Field in Marketing.

Busted, broke

Busted is a nonstandard word for *broke.*

> I *broke* (not: *busted*) the stapled printouts into two sections.

Can, may

Can refers to the ability to do something.

> *Can* she run four miles before dinner? (This is a question about someone's ability to run.)

Years ago I asked someone in Central Park, "Can I keep walking on this path and get to the West Side?" Apparently, the man I asked was sensitive to the nuances in English. His reply was, "Oh, you can walk on this path all right, but you won't get to the West Side."

May refers to permission.

> *May* she run four miles before dinner? (This is a question about whether someone has permission to run.)

The distinction between *can* and *may* is not often observed in everyday speech.

Cannot help but

Delete *but.*

> I *cannot help* (not: *cannot help but*) objecting to your argument.

Capital, capitol

Capitol: the name of a building.

> The *Capitol* in Washington looks like an *O* from above.

Capital: all other uses.

> You need *capital* to start a business.
>
> Albany is New York's *capital.*
>
> Each sentence begins with a *capital* letter.

Censor, censure

Censor is to remove from view.

> The sexy scenes were *censored.*

Censure is to condemn or criticize strongly.

> I cannot *censure* her behavior, for I feel she was justified.

Choose, chose

Choose: present tense (rhymes with *blues*)

> I like to *choose* a different flavor of yogurt every day.

Chose: past tense (rhymes with *hose*)

I *chose* strawberry yogurt yesterday.

Cite, site, sight

To *cite* is to *state*.

I can *cite* her reasons, but I don't understand them.

A *site* is a *place*.

He went to the excavation site.

Sight refers to *vision*.

It was love at first *sight*.

Clothes, cloths

Clothes (rhymes with *toes*)

He wears beautiful *clothes*.

Cloths (rhymes with *moths*) refers to material.

His clothes are made from beautiful *cloths*.

Compliment, complement

Compliment means to *praise*. Hint: You comp*li*ment things you *li*ke.

I *complimented* the manager on her efficiency.

Complimentary means *free*. Hint: You give free things to people you *li*ke.

He gave us *complimentary* tickets for the game.

Complement means to go well with or to complete. Hint: Com-pl*e*mentary things compl*e*te.

Red wine *complements* meat dishes.

Comprise, compose

These two words are not synonymous. To *comprise* is to *include*.

> Her territory *comprises* (includes) the North and Northeast. (The whole *comprises* the parts.)

To *compose* is to *make up*.

> The North and Northeast *compose* (make up) her territory. (The parts *compose* the whole.)
>
> *or*
>
> Her territory *is composed of* (is made up of) the North and Northeast. (The whole *is composed of* the parts.)

A common error: The territory *is comprised of* the North and Northeast. Do not use that expression.

Conscious, conscience

Conscious means *aware of*.

> I wasn't *conscious* of that habit.

Conscience is an inner sense of right and wrong.

> Let your *conscience* be your guide.

Continuous, continual

Continuously means *unceasingly, without a break*.

> The baby cried *continuously* for twenty minutes.

Continually means *recurring frequently*.

> The phone in the customer service area rings *continually*.

This distinction is not always observed.

Could of, may of, might of, should of, would of

All these are incorrect. When we speak, we sometimes fail to pronounce the *have* in *could have* and instead pronounce it *could of*. However, in both speaking and writing, the correct words are *could have*.

> I *could have* (not *could of*) given you the answer.

Council, counsel, consul, console

Council: an *official group.*

> The City *Council* met last night.

Counsel: to *give advice.*

> His lawyer *counseled* him not to speak to the press.

Consul: a *foreign representative.*

> The Panamanian *consul* is in Washington, D.C.

Console: comfort.

> When we lost the account, we tried to *console* the sales rep.

Criterion, criteria

Criterion means a *standard. Criterion* is singular; *criteria* is plural.

> The only *criterion* for the job is masochism.

> There are three *criteria* for being an offensive lineman: weight, speed, and agility.

Currently, presently

Currently means *now.*

> I am *currently* working on the Sherman file.

Presently combined with a present-tense verb also means *now.*

I am *presently* working on the Sherman file.

Presently combined with a future-tense verb means *soon.*

I will presently work on the Watson file.

The words *now* and *soon* can be used instead of *presently.*

Datum, data

The dictionary states that *datum* is singular; *data* is plural. However, *data* is commonly used as both a singular and plural word. Scientists, however, maintain the distinction between these words.

The data *is* (or: *are*) inconclusive. (everyday use)

The datum *is* inconclusive. (scientific use)

The data *are* inconclusive. (scientific use)

Desert, dessert

Dessert is what you eat; you spell it with two *s*'s because you always want seconds.

The other uses have one *s* only.

Don't *desert* me.

The caravan crossed the *desert.*

Different from, different than

The preferred form is *different from* except when using this phrase would lead to wordiness.

The results were *different from* (not: *different than*) what we had expected.

However, *She is a different person now than she used to be* is preferable to *She is a different person now from the person she used to be.*

Discreet, discrete

Discreet means *careful* in one's conduct, including the ability to maintain silence on private matters.

> She is a *discreet* person; you can confide in her.

Discrete refers to separate units.

> We have three *discrete* problems with this project.

Disinterested, uninterested

Disinterested means *impartial* or *unbiased*.

> The judge should be *disinterested* in each trial.

Uninterested means *not interested in*.

> Sheila was *uninterested* in physics.
>
> or (*more naturally*)
>
> Sheila was *not interested* in physics.

We want judges who are *disinterested*, but not *uninterested*, in the matters that come before them.

Do, due

Do not confuse *do* (You *do* something to me) with *due*, meaning when something must occur (The paper is *due* next Tuesday) or why something happens (Their success is *due* to hard work).

Due to, because of

See *Because, due to*.

Due to the fact that

Wordy for *because*.

Each and every one

Wordy for *each* or *every.*

> **Wordy:**
> *Each and every one* of the accounts must be reconciled.
>
> **Preferred:**
> *Each* account must be reconciled.
>
> *Every* account must be reconciled.

Elicit, illicit

To *elicit* is to *call forth.*

> The professor tried unsuccessfully to *elicit* some questions from the students.

Illicit means *unlawful* and usually is used to describe something morally reprehensible.

> Drug selling is an *illicit* activity.

Emigrate, immigrate

Emigrate means to go *out of* a country.

> The new citizen *emigrated* from Russia.

Immigrate means to *enter into* a country.

> That same new citizen *immigrated* to the United States.

Enthused

The preferred word is *enthusiastic.* Beware: Many careful speakers and writers strongly object to the word *enthused,* although others claim it is a legitimate word.

> **Frowned upon:**
> She is enthused.

Preferred:
She is enthusiastic.

Epigram, epigraph, epitaph, epithet

The first three words have to do with writing or inscriptions.
An *epigram* is a witty *saying.*

> Nothing so needs reforming as other people's habits.
> (Mark Twain)

An *epigraph* is a *quotation* inscribed on a building or statue, or a quotation at the beginning of a book or chapter.

> The U.S. Post Office has this *epigraph* in huge letters: "Neither snow nor rain nor heat nor gloom of night stays these couriers from the swift completion of their appointed rounds."

An *epitaph* is an *inscription* on a tomb.

> The hypochondriac left instructions that his *epitaph* read, "See, I told you I was sick!"

Epithet originally meant a nickname or description of a person, used after a person's name, such as Richard the Lionhearted or Jimmy the Greek. It is now commonly used to mean a word or expression communicating hatred or disdain.

> Bill—that good-for-nothing bum.

Et al.

A Latin expression (*et alii*) meaning *and other people.* Use *et al.* instead of *etc.* in a list of people.

> Smith *et al.* wrote the article.

Etc., and etc.

Etc. is an abbreviation for the Latin phrase *et cetera,* which means *and other things.* By writing *and etc.,* you are actually saying *and and other things.*

Books, magazines, pamphlets, *etc.*, (not: *and etc.*) were left on the table.

When *etc.* ends a series of items, put a comma before and after the *etc.*

Everywheres

Use *everywhere*, not *everywheres*. (See *Anywheres.*)

Ex, former

Use *ex* to indicate the person who immediately precedes the current holder of a position. *Former* refers to all those who held that position earlier than the *ex.*

Susan's *ex*-husband gets along well with her four *former husbands.*

The president, the *ex*-president, and *former* presidents (not: *All the ex-presidents*) always attend funerals of heads of state.

Explicit, implicit

Explicit means *stated outright.*

I left explicit instructions.

Implicit means unstated but *implied.*

I said nothing. She understood that the implicit answer was no.

Farther, further

Farther refers to distance. Use *farther* when the distance can be measured in miles, feet, inches, and so forth.

She runs *farther* than I do.

Use *further* when the distance can't be measured. *Further* refers to degree or extent.

Let's discuss this problem *further*.

Fewer, less

Use *fewer* for things you can count.

The second draft had *fewer* (not: *less*) errors than the first one.

This dish has *fewer* (not: *less*) calories than I thought.

Exception: Use *less than* with plural nouns that refer to time periods, amounts of money, but not people.

less than a dozen years ago

less than a dollar

fewer than eighty sales representatives

Use *less* for things you can't count.

The staff is *less* gloomy since profits went up.

The new reduced-fat cookies have *less* fat but the same number of calories as the regular cookies.

Note: The expressions *50 words or less* and *10 items or less* are incorrect but so commonly used they are considered idioms. (Idioms are usages that violate the rules but are nevertheless accepted by the authorities.)

Finalize

See *Prioritize, finalize,* and other *-ize* words.

Flammable, inflammable

These two words mean *easy to set fire to. Flammable* is the better choice.

For all intensive purposes

This is a misstatement of *for all intents and purposes.*

Fourth, forth

Fourth refers to *four.*

> She's the *fourth* person who made that comment.

Forth refers to direction.

> Stop going back and *forth.*

Beware: Fortieth, not *fourtieth,* is the way to spell *40th.*

From off, off from, off of

These expressions are redundant. Do not use *of* or *from* with *off.*

> I bought the gadget *from* (not: *off from* or *from off*) a dealer.

> The pen fell *off* (not: *off of*) the desk.

Good, well

Which is correct?

> The machine works *good.*
> The machine works *well.*

Correct:
> The machine works *well.*

To understand why this is the correct choice, you must understand these points.

Point 1: *Good* describes people or things.

> She's a *good* person.
> That's a *good* point.

Point 2: *Well* describes how someone or something does an action.

John speaks *well.*

The machine works *well.*

Point 3: After any form of the verbs *to be, to smell,* or *to taste,* the correct choice is *good.* There is one exception.

This is a *good* idea.

Rudolf is *good.*

I feel *good.* (This means I am in good spirits.)

Exception: Use *I am well* or *I feel well* to refer to the state of your health.

Hanged, hung

Use *hanged* to refer to executions, *hung* in other uses.

The assassin was *hanged* from a tree.

The hammock was *hung* in the backyard.

I *hung* my hat in the hall.

Have, of

See *Could of, may of, might of, should of, would of.*

Here, hear

Hear means to listen. (You *hear* with your *ears.*) *Here* means in this place. (*Here* is the opposite of *there.*)

Hisself

Nonstandard. Use *himself.*

Hopefully

Grammarians have arguments about the use of this word. Some say it can be used only to mean *with hope,* as it does in this sentence:

> He looked *hopefully* at the envelope containing his bonus.

They reject

> *Hopefully,* we'll finish the proposal on time.

because here *hopefully* does not mean *With hope we'll finish the proposal on time;* it means *It is hoped that* or *I hope that we'll finish the proposal on time.*

Other grammarians see no reason to condemn *Hopefully, we'll finish the proposal on time*—and neither do I.

Hopefully, this issue will disappear.

If, whether

Strictly speaking, *if* means *supposing that.*

> *If* it rains, we will postpone the fair.

Whether is used to introduce an alternative.

> I haven't decided *whether* or not to attend (not: *if* I will attend).

However, this distinction is not commonly maintained.

Imply, infer

To *imply* is to *suggest* something without stating it directly.

> The customer *implied* that our product was reasonably priced when he said it was within his budget.

To *infer* is to *conclude* from something a person says.

> I *inferred* that I'd gotten the job when the personnel director complimented me on my extensive job experi-

ence and said that I would be receiving a call from her within the next few days.

In lieu of

In lieu of means *in place of.* Do not use it to mean *in view of.*

> We will accept a letter of agreement *in lieu* of a formal contract.

In regards to, with regards to

These expressions are incorrect. Use instead:

> I need to speak with you *in regard to* (or *with regard to*) Mr. Young's account. (No *s.*)

or better yet:

> I need to speak with you *about* Mr. Young's account.

Incidently

A misspelling of the word *incidentally.*

Individual, person, persons, people

Use *individual* when referring to a single human being, in contrast to a group.

> One *individual* on the jury held out for an acquittal.

Use *people*, rather than *persons*, for the plural of *person.*

> She gave me a list of the *people* (not: *persons* or *individuals*) who will attend the dinner.

(*Persons* seems to be preferred by those who write those elevator signs that say *Not safe for occupancy by more than 20 persons.*)

Initiate, instigate

To *initiate* is to *start*. (It is related to the word *initial*, meaning first.)

> The project will be *initiated* by the end of the year.

To *instigate* is to *start something going*, usually something unpleasant.

> He *instigated* (not: *initiated*) a rebellion among the sales reps against the new commission plan.

Irregardless, regardless

Irregardless is not a word. Use *regardless*, since *regardless* means *without regard*. If you say *irregardless*, you are actually saying *without without regard*.

Its, it's

See Rule 21, Note, page 76.

Kind of a

Incorrect, use *kind of* instead.

> This *kind of* (not: *kind of a*) job can be done easily.

Knew, new

Knew is related to the word *knowledge*. *New* refers to age.

> He *knew* the answer.

> He *knew* we wanted a *new* car.

Later, latter, last

Later refers to time.

> Can we do that *later*?

Latter refers to the second of two items.

> Mr. Jones and Mr. Smith work here. The *latter* can speak with you now.

Last is used when more than two things are mentioned.

> The file cabinets, the work stations, and the chairs are on order. The *last* will arrive next week.

Leave, let

Leave means *go away*.

> I have to *leave* you now.

Let means *allow*.

> *Let* (not: *leave*) me show you how the system works.

Note: Leave me alone and *let me alone* are both acceptable if you want to be by yourself. In the first, you are asking the person to leave; in the second, you are asking permission to be left alone. Not much of a difference.

Lie, lay

Much confusion abounds over how to use these two words. Most people do not realize they are two separate words. Here's how each is used in the various tenses. (Note that *lay* occurs on both lists. That's the reason for the confusion.)

Lie: to *recline*—what a person or an animal does

> I *lie* down on my couch every day at 3:00 P.M. (present tense)

> I *lay* down yesterday at 3:00 P.M. (past tense)

> I *have lain* down every day at 3:00 P.M. for the past 20 years. (something done repeatedly in the past and then continued into the present)

> I *will lie* down at 3:00 P.M. (future tense)

Lay: to *place*—what people do to things

> I *lay* the mail on his desk every day. (present tense)
>
> I *laid* the mail on his desk yesterday. (past tense)
>
> I *have laid* the mail on his desk for the past 20 years. (something done repeatedly in the past and then continued into the present)
>
> I *will lay* the mail on his desk tomorrow. (future tense)

Like, as

Strict grammarians insist that *as* be used to link two sentences together. This rule is seldom followed in spoken English, in which *like* seems to be squeezing out *as*.

Here, for the record, is the difference between *as* and *like* in formal usage.

As is used as a link between two sentences. Note that in both sentences, a subject and verb follow the word *as.*

> I'm treating you *as* (not: *like*) I would like to be treated.
>
> He looks *as* (not: *like*) his father did at the same age.
>
> She does the same things *as* you did at that age.
>
> It looks *as if* (not: *like*) it will rain.

Like is used when a subject and verb do not follow.

> She looks *like* you.
>
> I need someone *like* you on my side.

Loose, lose

Things that are *loose* are not tight.

> She lost weight and her clothes got *loose.*

Things that you *lose* cannot be found.

> It's better to *lose* your wallet than your confidence.

May of

See *Could of, may of, might of, should of, would of.*

Media, medium

Media refers to channels of communication and is therefore plural.

The *media are* (not: *is*) covering the trial closely.

Medium refers to one channel.

We decided that radio would be the best advertising *medium* for our new product.

Might could

Might could is not standard English.

I *might* (not: *might could*) give you the change.

Might of

See *Could of, may of, might of, should of, would of.*

Militate, mitigate

These two totally unrelated words are often misused.
To *mitigate* is to *lessen*.

We tried to *mitigate* the child's grief over his lost teddy bear by telling him we would buy him a new one.

We often hear this word used in the *-ing* form.

I was late, but there was a *mitigating* circumstance: My car broke down.

To *militate* is to *act against.*

His mediocre performance appraisals *militated* against his chances of becoming a supervisor.

Mine's

Incorrect. People who say *mine's* are making the word *mine,* which means *belonging to me,* doubly possessive: *That is mine's* means *That belongs to me belongs to me.*

Moral, morale

Moral has two unrelated meanings.
   Moral refers to ethics or correct behavior.

   The country needs more *moral* people.

Moral is also used to mean the main point.

   The *moral* of the story is never put off to tomorrow what you can put off to the day after tomorrow.

Morale refers to spirit.

   We need to increase employee *morale.*

Myself

See *A Special Note About Myself* (page 128).

Nauseous, nauseated

Many heavy-duty grammarians claim that one must say *I am nauseated* rather than *I am nauseous* or *I feel nauseous.* However, the *Random House Unabridged Dictionary* claims we can use any of these expressions.

Notorious, famous

Notorious means *famous for negative reasons.*

   Al Capone was *notorious* for his crimes.

Famous means just plain *famous*.

> My boss is *famous* (not: *notorious*) for giving big bonuses.

On account of

Wordy. Use *because*.

Orient, orientate

To *orient* is to *introduce someone to something*.

> You will need to *orient* the new employee to some of our strange office customs.

Use it rather than *orientate*.

Outside of

Of is redundant.

> The ships were *outside* the fishing zone. (not: The ships were *outside of* the fishing zone.)

Owing to the fact that

Wordy. Use *because*.

Passed, past

Passed means *went by* (a verb).

> She *passed* me on the street.

Past refers to a time.

> I don't think I want to know about your *past*.

People, persons

Use *people* rather than *persons* in everyday situations. (See *Individual*.)

Percent, percentage

Use *percent* if a specific number is given.

>Forty *percent* of the participants enjoyed the program.

Use *percentage* if an indefinite word, such as *large, small, significant,* is given.

>A significant *percentage* (not: *percent*) of stocks are worthless.

Principal, principle

Principal has three different meanings:
A person who is in charge of a school.

>I still remember my grade school principal. (Tip: The princi*pal* is your *pal.*)

The main part of something.

>The principal requirement for success is persistence, though talent and good luck are also important.

A sum of money.

>A mortgage consists of interest plus principal.

Principle is a basic truth or belief. (Remember: A princip*le* is a ru*le.*)

>This was the principal's principal *principle:* "Get to school!"

Prioritize, finalize, and other -ize words

Some heavy-duty grammarians argue against the words *prioritize* and *finalize,* while others find them perfectly acceptable. I side with the latter. Isn't it more concise to say, "Let's prioritize our tasks," than, "Let's put our tasks in order of priority"?

Quiet, quite

Quiet means *without sound.*

A *quiet* evening at home is what I want.

Quite means *almost completely.*

I'm *quite* content.

Real, really

Real is an adjective, so it must describe a noun.

The omelette is made with *real* cheese.

In everyday speech we often hear *real* used as an adverb: *He's real good with people.* This is incorrect. The correct usage is *He is really good with people.*

Really is an adverb and thus can only describe a verb, an adverb, or an adjective.

He is really good with people (*Good* is an adjective. [See adjectives and adverbs on page 239 in the Glossary.])

The reason is because

Avoid this phrase because it is redundant. *Because* means *for the reason that.* Use *the reason is that* or revise the sentence.

Incorrect:

The reason for the confusion is *because* the instructions were not clear.

Correct:

The reason for the confusion is *that* the instructions were not clear.

The confusion was due to the unclear instructions.

The confusion was created by the unclear instructions.

The unclear instructions caused confusion.

Respectfully, respectively

Respectfully means *with respect* or *full of respect.*

> She spoke of him *respectfully.*

Respectively means *each in the order given.*

> The authors of the first and second plays were Shakespeare and Bacon, *respectively.*

Retroactive to, retroactive from

Retroactive from is incorrect.

> The pay raise is *retroactive to* the first of the month.

Rise, raise

Rise means *get up.*

> Every day on the bus, I *rise* and give my seat to elderly people. (present tense)

> I *rose* and gave my seat to an elderly person yesterday. (past tense)

> I *have risen* every day for the past twenty years to give my seat to an elderly person. (present perfect tense)

> I *will rise* and give my seat to an elderly person tomorrow. (future tense)

Raise means *move something in an upward direction.*

> I *raise* my hand at 3:00 and yell, "Break time!" (present tense)

> I *raised* my hand at 3:00 yesterday and yelled, "Break time!" (past tense)

> I *have raised* my hand every day at 3:00 and yelled, "Break time!" for the past twenty years. (present perfect tense)

I *will raise* my hand tomorrow at 3:00 and yell, "Break time!" (future tense)

Said

Do not use *said* to mean *this* or *it*.

Incorrect:

The performance appraisal is to be completed and signed. Said document must be delivered to me by 5:00 P.M.

Correct:

The performance appraisal is to be completed and signed. It must be delivered to me by 5:00 P.M.

Same

Do not use *same* to mean *it*.

Incorrect:

The performance appraisal is to be completed and signed. The same must be delivered to me by 5:00 P.M.

Correct:

The performance appraisal is to be completed and signed. It must be delivered to me by 5:00 P.M.

Scarcely

Since this word is negative in meaning, do not use it with another negative.

He *scarcely* recognized (not: *didn't scarcely recognize*) me.

Serve, service

Things are *serviced*.

The car was *serviced* by a reputable mechanic.

People are *served*.

We are proud of the way we *serve* (not: *service*) our clients.

Set, sit

To *sit* is to *seat oneself*.

I'll *sit* down here and wait for you.

Won't you *sit* by the fire with me?

To *set* is to *place something*.

I will *set* the dish on the table.

Generally, to *set* is to place; to *sit* is to take a position of rest, e.g., to sit in a chair. Therefore, *Set right down until I get back* is incorrect (though commonly heard in certain parts of the United States).

Shall, will

At one time careful speakers and writers made a distinction between these two words. Today, however, no distinction need be made.

So, so that

When *so* means *therefore,* it requires a comma (see Rule 1, page 35.)

I want to leave now, *so* I will say good-bye to the hostess.

So that means *in order that* and does not require a comma.

I will say good-bye to the hostess *so that* (or *so*) I can go home.

Stationary, stationery

Something is *stationary* if it doesn't move. Stationary things just stand there.

Stationery is what you write on. Stationery is for writing letters.

Than, then

Than is used for comparison.

> She was taller *than* he was.

Then refers to time.

> *Then* five years passed, and he was taller *than* she was.

That, which

The distinction between these two words is fading. Careful writers use *that* to introduce essential information, *which* for additional information. *Which* clauses are set aside in commas, *that* phrases or clauses are not. (For an explanation of essential and additional (nonessential) information, see pages 50–52.)
Either of the sentences below is correct; the *that* and the *which* and the punctuation change the way the sentence is read.

> The letter *that* must be mailed by 5:00 is on Sara's desk.

> The Clark letter, *which* is on Sara's desk, must be mailed by 5:00.

There, their, they're

There refers to a place.

> We eat *there* every day. There is the opposite of here.

Their means *belonging to them.*

> They put *their* briefcases in the closet.

They're is a contraction meaning *they are.*

> Don't worry; *they're* always on time.

This here, those here, these ones, them there, that there

Nonstandard. Delete *here, ones, there.*

Two, too, to

Two: 2.

> She had *two* concerns about my proposal.

Too: Also; excessively.

> I want a double fudge brownie *too.*

> Her dog was *too* friendly; he jumped up and kissed the burglar.

To: All other uses.

> It's time *to* move on *to* the next item.

Uninterested, disinterested

See *Disinterested, uninterested.*

Utilize

Plain old *use* is just as good.

> We need to *use* (not: *utilize*) the new software to make slides.

Verb Problems

Here are some serious errors.

Incorrect:	Correct:
I should have went	I should have gone
I seen him	I saw him
I done the work	I did the work
I had wrote	I had written
It don't work right	It doesn't work right

If you use any of the incorrect forms, you are speaking in a way that may be considered correct in a particular community, but is considered nonstandard and incorrect in the larger community.

Weather, whether

Weather is the *climate:* good, bad, sunny, rainy, and so forth.

The *weather* has been exceptional.

Whether is related to the expression *whether or not*.

I can't decide *whether* to accept the invitation.

Were, where

Were is a verb, the simple past tense or a helping verb.

What *were* you doing in my files?

Where refers to a place.

Where *are* you?

Where's he at? is redundant. Just say, "*Where is he?*"

Where, when, a situation where, a problem where, is where, is when

These phrases are incorrect. Do not use them.

Incorrect:
> We have *a situation where* (or: *a problem where*) a person misfiles a tape and then no one else can find it.

Correct:
> We have *a situation* (or: *a problem*) *in which* a person misfiles a tape and then no one else can find it.

Incorrect:
> Employee orientation *is where* (or: *is when*) new employees learn about the policies and practices of the organization.

Correct:

Employee orientation *is* a two-hour class for new employees in which the policies and practices of the organization are explored.

Who, Whom in questions

Is it *Who should we contact?* or *Whom should we contact?*

To determine which is correct, turn the question into a statement. Then try each sentence out—once with *he,* once with
him—and select the best fit.

1. Turn the question into a statement, using *who* or *whom.*

   We should contact *who.*

   We should contact *whom.*

2. Substitute *he* for *who, him* for *whom.*

   We should contact *he.*

   We should contact *him.*

Correct:

Whom should we contact?

Who, Whom in statements

Is it *You know who is the best person for the job* or *You know whom is the
best person for the job?*

To determine which is correct, isolate the part of the sentence
that starts with *who* or *whom.* Then try out each part—using *he*
for *who* and *him* for *whom*—and select the best fit.

1. Isolate the part of the sentence that starts with *who* or
   whom.

   Who is best for the job.

   Whom is best for the job.

2. Substitute *he* for *who, him* for *whom.*

He is best for the job.

Him is best for the job.

Correct:
You know *who* is best for the job.

One more time—is it *You should vote for whoever is the most qualified* or *You should vote for whomever is the most qualified?*

1. Isolate the part of the sentence that starts with *whoever* or *whomever.*

Whoever is the most qualified.

Whomever is the most qualified.

2. Substitute *he* for *whoever, him* for *whomever.*

He is the most qualified.

Him is the most qualified.

Correct:
You should vote for *whoever* is the most qualified.

Who's, whose

Who's is a contraction for *who is.*

Who's registered for the class?

Whose means belonging to someone.

Whose briefcase is this? (*To whom* does this briefcase belong?)

Woman, women

One *woman,* two *women.*

You're, your

You're is a contraction.

>*You're* the best! (*You are* the best!)

Your is a possessive form.

>Is that *your* house? (Does it belong to you?)

Words That Are Easy to ~~Mispell~~ Misspell

A

accept
accommodate
acknowledgment
all right
appraisal

B

bankruptcy
basically
budget
bureaucracy

C

calendar
category
ceiling
changeable
cite (to mention)
coefficient
collateral
commitment
compatible

concurrence
consensus
correspondence

D

deferment
deterrent
dilemma
discernible

E

eighth
embarrass
equipment
equipped

F

familiar
feasibility
February
fiduciary
forfeit

G

gauge
grammar
grievance

H

height
hierarchy

I

illicit
impetus
incessant

J

judgment

K

kilometer
knowledge

L

liable
lieu

M

maintenance
maneuver
mediocre
microprocessor
milieu
monitor

N

necessary

O

occasion
occurrence
overrun

P

permissible
precede
preferred
prerogative

prevalent
privilege
proceed
protocol
publicly

Q

questionnaire

R

rapport
reciprocal
recommend
recurrence
referred
relevant
remittance
rescind

S

scenario
site (place)
succeed
supersede
synopsis

T

threshold
tomorrow
trafficking
treasurer

U

unanimous

V

verbatim
versatile
vice versa

W

waiver
withheld

Y

yield

Z

zero-based

Simple Business Verbs You Should Know

access	demonstrate	implement	process
accumulate	deputize	indicate	propose
activate	designate	individualize	recommend
analyze	develop	initiate	reconcile
approve	distribute	innovate	reconfigure
arbitrate	document	integrate	resolve
articulate	emphasize	interface	review
augment	emulate	involve	revise
brainstorm	energize	maintain	streamline
commit	enhance	manipulate	support
communicate	establish	maximize	sustain
complement	evaluate	minimize	transform
complete	expedite	mobilize	update
concur	explain	modify	upgrade
configure	explore	motivate	validate
confirm	facilitate	organize	verify
consider	forecast	orient	
coordinate	highlight	persuade	
delegate	identify	prioritize	

Formatting of Letters and Memos

Letters on Company Stationery

Cats Incorporated
1123 FISHY LANE
ALLEYVILLE, MO 12345

.... (4–8 lines)

May 2, 1990

.... (2 lines)

Mr. Arthur Bowser
President
Doggy Ventures
456 Dog Run
Kennel Town, NJ 00007

.... (2 lines)

Dear Mr. Bowser:

.... (2 lines)
Thank you for ordering 20 barrels of Happy Tyme Litter. Please let us know how the puppies do. This could be a real breakthrough for animal comfort stations across the country.

.... (2 lines)
I'm enclosing our new catalog, *Cat Stuff Dogs Love.* We'll be happy to give you a 25% discount on all multiple orders.

.... (2 lines)
Sincerely,

.... (4 lines)
Sam Kitty
Sales Manager

.... (2 lines)
Enc.

Memos

Cats Incorporated
Interoffice Memo

To: Minnie Mouse
From: Sam Kitty
Date: May 4, 1991
Subject: Marketing Cat Products for Dogs

. . . . (3 lines)
Please send Arthur Bowser sample cans of Tasty Tuna and a box of Yummy Tummy Balls immediately. I think we've got a "live" one. (See attached copy of my letter to Mr. Bowser.)

Glossary

Adjective—a word that describes a noun.

> The cat with the *beautiful, soft* fur destroyed everything in sight.

> *Beautiful* and *soft* describe the noun *fur.*

Adverb—a word that describes a verb, an adjective, or another adverb.

> Describing a verb . . .

> > The cat with the beautiful, soft fur *quickly* destroyed everything in sight.

> *Quickly* describes the verb *destroyed.* It describes how everything was destroyed.

> Describing an adjective . . .

> > The cat with the *extremely* beautiful, *seductively* soft fur quickly destroyed everything in sight.

> *Extremely* describes the adjective *beautiful.* It describes how beautiful the cat was. *Seductively* describes the adjective soft. It describes how soft the fur was.

> Describing another adverb . . .

> > The cat with the extremely beautiful, seductively soft fur *very* quickly destroyed everything in sight.

Very describes the adverb *quickly*. It describes how quickly everything was destroyed.

Clause—A group of words containing both a subject and a verb. Some clauses can stand by themselves; others cannot.

> The bus stopped when the driver came to the intersection.

The bus stopped could stand by itself as a complete sentence. *When the driver came to the intersection* is a clause. Some sentences are made up of two clauses, each of which could stand alone.

> *Phil (subject)* listened *(verb)* carefully to the instructions, and *he (subject)* then ignored *(verb)* them.

Cliff-hanger or Cliff-hanger Clause—A group of words containing a subject and a verb that can't stand alone. It precedes a clause that can stand alone.

> When the driver came to the intersection, the bus stopped.

When the driver came to the intersection is a cliff-hanger.

These words often introduce a cliff-hanger: *after, although (though), as (as if), because, before, if, since, unless, how, when, where, while, until, so that.*

Noun—The name of a person, place, or thing.

> The *administrator* explained the *procedure* to me.
> The *reason* for the *change* was hard to understand.

Phrase—A group of words. One kind of phrase is a prepositional phrase.

Prepositional phrases begin with a preposition. Common prepositions include *about, after, against, among, at, before, between, by, concerning, during, except, for, from, in, into, near, of, off, on, over, since, to, under, with, without.*

Each prepositional phrase is italicized.

Please speak *with me immediately.*

During lunch, we discussed everything *except the price.*

We cannot send information *concerning the product.*

Pronoun—A word that takes the place of a noun.

Jane looked at the picture; *she* loved *it.*

She takes the place of Jane; *it* takes the place of *the picture.*

Subject—A word that defines what the sentence is about.

Rita enjoys basking in the sun.

The enormous box was delivered at about 4:30 P.M.

Verb—A word that describes an action or merely the fact that something simply is.

Some verbs are easy to picture:

Alan *tripped* on the welcome mat.

Myra *handed* me a folder.

I *received* the information yesterday.

Some are not:

I finally *remembered* her name.

I *felt* strange as I entered the large, empty room.

They *think* that is the best strategy.

It is especially hard to recognize verbs that are forms of *to be* and *to have* because they don't *do* anything. However, these verbs, often called state-of-being verbs, are full-fledged verbs.

Barbara *is* my best friend.

The decision *will be* difficult.

His decision *was* a difficult one.

I *have* a great idea.

He *has* a car just like yours.

Bibliography

Bernstein, Theodore. *The Careful Writer: A Modern Guide to English Usage.* New York: Atheneum, 1965.

Dumond, Val. *Grammar for Grownups.* New York: HarperCollins Publishers, 1993.

Fowler, H. Ramsey, and Jane E. Aaron. *The Little Brown Handbook.* 5th ed. New York: HarperCollins Publishers, 1992.

Hodges, John C., and Mary E. Whitten. *Harbrace College Handbook.* 10th ed. New York: Harcourt Brace Jovanovich, 1986.

Sabin, William A. *The Gregg Reference Manual.* 7th ed. Lake Forest, Ill.: Glencor Macmillan/McGraw Hill, 1992.

Skillin, Marjorie E. *Words into Type.* 3rd ed. Englewood Cliffs, N.J.: Prentice-Hall, 1974.

University of Chicago Press. *The Chicago Manual of Style.* 14th ed. Chicago, Ill.: The University of Chicago Press, 1993.

Venolia, Jan. *Write Right!* 2nd ed. Berkeley, Calif.: Ten Speed Press, 1989.

Warriner, John E. *English Grammar and Composition.* 4th rev. ed. New York: Harcourt Brace Jovanovich, 1984.

Index

If you would like more information about how you can bring an ActionGrammar or ActionWriting program to your company, please contact:

Joanne Feierman
Seminars in Communication
115 East 92nd Street
New York, New York 10128
(212) 427-7395